I0476251

THE SMART MANAGER

By Tony Narams. Ph.d

All Rights Reserved

Copyright 2011 Tony

Narams. Ph.d

BOOK's DESCRIPTION

THIS BOOK IS ALL YOU NEED

TO UNDERSTAND

THE PRACTICE OF MANAGEMENT!

A classic since its First publication, The Practice of Management (**The Smart Manger**) was the first book to look at management as a whole and being a manager as a separate responsibility. The Practice of Management created the discipline of modern management practices. Readable, fundamental, and basic, it remains an essential book for students, aspiring managers, and seasoned professionals.

It's written in Simple Point form for easy reference.

This is the same script that top level managers use! It has been in use in over 5000 renowned business management schools around the world!

WORTH OVER $135,000 OF BASIC MANAGEMENT COURSE FOR TOP LEVEL MANAGERS!

INTRODUCTION

Management Practice is a sequence of core and elective courses that integrate the concepts and tools of the other coursework, and Help Bridge from the classroom to the workplace.

This book will prepare you (its students) for Readiness to enter the real world of cooperate, form internship to permanent management position. It will assist you face complex problems and help you figure out solutions to the dire challenges you will face as a Manager. Through this program you will develop the confidence to address the ambiguity of the real world and earn the tools to navigate and address messy unstructured problems. You will also acquire 'the people skills' that will enable you manage and organize effectively projects, teams, etc, and strengthen your communication skills to develop and sell high-quality, action-oriented solutions.

This training WILL ENABLE YOU apply your core skills by integrating them with three interconnected work processes valued by the marketplace:

1. Effective team work

2. Quality problem solving

3. Persuasive communication

Thus becoming a smart manager!

OTHER BENEFITS OF THIS COURSE BOOK:

The four following are other benefits –but not limited to:-

1. Managing Projects and Teams

Getting things done is essential for every successful business professional. The most challenging real-world problems involve multiple issues and usually require the talents and energies of multiple people. Students learn methods for planning and facilitating teamwork, and managing the work required to guide complex, multi-part projects. Field projects help students practice their skills in managing team dynamics, facilitating creativity, resolving conflicts, and giving and receiving feedback.

2. Solving Problems

Real-world problems don't always arrive well-structured; some don't even announce their arrival. Students learn how to identify critical questions, decompose them into manageable and logical parts, and then create the work flows required to analyze those questions. Critical analytical thinking skills are used to arrive at good insights and recommendations that are grounded in good logic and solid evidence.

3. Communicating and Persuading

Creating value in the real world requires people to take action. Students gain the skills and confidence to communicate objectives, plans and proposals in a convincing and knowledgeable manner, in order to drive change. This component of Management Practice strengthens a wide variety of oral and written communication techniques. Focus is placed on developing an authentic style, interviewing experts, listening, asking strong questions, and story-telling to meet the needs of organizations.

4. Management Practice Electives

The slate of management practice Electives spans a wide range of professional interests and directions, and it changes and evolves with the needs of the market.

****

Note: this course book is written in point form for easier reference and understanding. This is the same Course book that thousands of institutions are using to educate high level top managers!

Regards

Tony Narams.

CHAPTER ONE

INTRODUCTION TO MANAGEMENT

Definition of Management

The term management is defined in different ways by management writers.

All definitions of management achieve the same goal although they are differently defined. Some of the definitions are:-

i. Management is the art and science of utilizing material and human resources to accomplish a desired objective.

ii. Management is the process of obtaining, deploying and utilizing a variety of essential resources to contribute to organization's success.

Management as an art

Management is an art because:-

i.   The process of management involves knowledge and skill.

ii.   Management requires empirical knowledge

iii.   When operating a manager enforces personal judgment

iv.   When operating a manager enforces intuition (power of mind)

v.   Each manager applies his management style

vi.   Management involves creativity.

Management as a Science

Management is a science because:-

i. When operating, a manager other times uses scientific tools.

ii. The principles of management have been developed through continuous observation and empirical verification.

iii. The principles of management are capable of universal application

iv. Management theories help to examine and evaluate alternative courses of action to resolve a given problem.

Characteristics of Management

i. Management is universal i.e. Management principles are applicable everywhere.

ii. Management is purposeful i.e. Management exists for achievement of objectives.

iii. Management is an integrative force i.e. Management is about coordination of individual effort into team effort

iv. Management is a social process i.e Management is done by people and concerns interpersonal relations. The human factor is an important element in management.

v. Management is multi disciplinary

i.e. Management has to deal with human behavior under dynamic conditions .

vi. Management is a continuous process i.e management processes have no limit

vii. Management is intangible

i.e Management is unseen or invisible force but its force is felt everywhere.

viii. Management is an art as well as a science

i.e Management contains a systematic body of theoretical knowledge and also involves the practical application of such knowledge aided by scientific tools such as computers, mobiles and many more tools.

Objectives of Management

1.   Organizational objectives:

    i.   Reasonable profits so as to give a fair return on the capital invested in the business.

    ii.   Survival and solvency of business continuity.

    iii. Growth and expansion of the enterprise.

    iv.   Improving reputation of the business.

    v.   Improving the goodwill of the business.

2.   Personal objectives: an organization consists of several persons who have their own objectives. These objectives are:

    i.   Fair remuneration for work performed

ii.   Reasonable working conditions

iii.   Opportunities for training and development

iv.   Participation in management and prosperity of the enterprise

v.   Reasonable security of service

3. Social objectives: management is also expected to be responsible to various groups outside the organization. It is expected to fulfill the objectives of society which include;

I. To offer high quality of goods and services

ii.   To charge Fair prices to consumers

iii. To enforce honesty and prompt payment of taxes to the government

iv. To enforce conservation of the environment and natural resources

v.   Fair dealings with suppliers, dealers and competitors

vi. To present ethical values of the society.

Goals of management are:

i.   Achievement of group goals

ii.   Optimum utilization of resources

iii.   Minimization of costs

iv.   Survival and growth

v.   Development of the nation

Chapter 1/2: ESSENTIAL NATURE OF TASKS
AND CONTRIBUTIONS OF MANAGERS

Essential nature of managerial work

i.   Management is practiced for the purpose of achieving organizational objectives.

ii.   Managers, the people in positions of authority make decisions to commit organizational resources. They get things done through people who are the key of all organizational resources.

iii.   Managers are liable to pay special attention to people (human resource) in terms of its acquisition, utilization, development and retention.

iv.   Managers must secure for staff additional resources in terms of materials, equipment and money to enable staff to be effective.

v.   For the managers to achieve the goals they set, they must execute the various functions of management which include forecasting, planning, directing, organizing, controlling and co-ordination.

vi.   Management only requires efficiency and effectiveness regardless of organization's philosophy e.g. capitalistic or socialistic.

Note: Efficiency means being procedural or orderly, systematic or methodical, while effectiveness means being result- oriented to achieve targets, standards, objectives and satisfaction as a measure of productivity.

Specifically, management is about three factors:-

    i.   Accomplishment of group objectives

       The manager converts the various resources (people, machines, materials, money, time and space) into useful enterprise.

    ii.   Efficient running of organization

       This is done by the manager providing appropriate leadership to those he leads. He should explain the purpose behind organizational goals and seek to involve the subordinates mentally and emotionally in the accomplishment of organizational goals

    iii. Sound organizational structure

       The manager must establish a pattern of authority (responsibility, relationship) and provide a proper environment for people to be productive.

The tasks and contributions of a manager:-

A manager performs various tasks and also makes many decisions to enable the organization perform effectively.

Tasks of a Manager

    i.   Fulfills the specific purpose and mission of the organization

    ii.   Makes work productive

    iii.   Manages social impacts and social responsibilities

Basic operations of the work of a manager

    i.   Sets objectives: Determines objectives and goals. For each objective and goal, describes what needs to be done to achieve these Objectives and goals.

    ii.   Organizes: Analyses the activities, decisions and relations required, classifies and divides work, creates organization structure and selects staff.

    iii.   Coordinates: Creates a team out of people responsible for various jobs.

    iv.   Develops people: Directs, encourages and trains.

    v.   Motives: Encourages people by rewarding them and managing them democratically

    vi.   Communicates: Gets in touch with every person so as to develop group cohesiveness.

Essential Skills of a Manager

Managers like any other person, must have skills that enable them to effectively perform their functions. For a manager to succeed, one must have the following skills;

i.   Technical skills

The manager must know how to operate equipment which will enable him to perform specific tasks within the organization.

Technical skills are very essential for operational managers.

ii.   Conceptual skills

This is the skill that enables the manager to see the whole organization as a single unit of operation, be able to visualize the interrelationship between different components of the organization and how they should collaborate in achieving its global mission.

The conceptual skill also enables the manager to deeply understand the external environment of the organization as well as the new possibilities, threats and challenges it presents to the organization.

iii.   Human relations skills

The ability to work effectively with others in a harmonious manner, this requires a sense of feeling for others, an appreciation of rights which is demonstrated by the way the managers interact with their subordinates, peers and superiors.

Chapter 1/3: THE ATTRIBUTES OF AN EFFECTIVE MANAGER

The success of a manager depends on many factors. To be successful in their work, managers are required to have and be able to enforce fully the following attributes:-

1.Knowledge and skills of management

Management is a fast developing field of knowledge. Managers today are faced by many environmental challenges. To effectively compete, managers have to learn new skills in management.

2.Empirical knowledge in management

To succeed in management, a manager is expected to have a hand on experience in management in his area of specialization.

3.Smart

Smartness is very essential in managerial jobs. Smartness enables the manager to be:

i.   Respected and supported by the superiors

ii.   Respected and guided by his peers

iii.   Respected and obeyed by his juniors

iv.   Trusted by customers

v.   Respected by the public

4.Impartial

A manager is supposed to be impartial. He is expected to be fair to everyone regardless of any other factors such as tribal, friendship, culture, etc.

5.Flexible

A manager should be flexible. The decision that a manager takes should not be influenced by external forces.

6.Honest

A manager is supposed to be honest. Honesty enables a manager to be trusted by his juniors. Employees working in an environment which has an honest manager tend to maximize their production.

7.Forward looking

Most people in life regret for their failure to achieve their targets. Managers are therefore advised to plan and set goals that should be achieved in a specified time.

8.Tactful

A manager is expected to be tactful when he performs his work. Most times managers differ with their juniors because they handle juniors untactful. A manager's job has very many demands which makes the manager stressed. A stressed manager easily loses their temper; it is, therefore advisable for a manager to handle staff and clients tactfully so as to create a harmonious working environment.

9.Social

A manager is supposed to be social to his staff. Most managers are unsocial to their staff. Interacting with staff is very important because the manager will know his staff well, an element which will enable the manager to appraise his staff democratically.

10.Friendly

A manager should be friendly, not only to his staff but also to customers and public.

Chapter 1/4: MANAGEMENT THEORIES AND CONCEPTS

A theory is a systematic grouping of independent concepts and principles that gives a framework that has together significant areas of knowledge. It is relevant in the field of management because it provides a means of classifying significant and pertinent management knowledge. When identifying an effective organization structure, there are a number of principles applied and which are inter-related. These principles have a predictive value to managers e.g. certain principles guide managers when delegating authority in an organization.

Theories and history of management are important to managers for the following reasons:-

·   History assists managers in understanding the current developments and avoids mistakes of the past.History and theory foster an understanding and appreciation of the current situation and development, also facilitate the prediction of future conditions

·   Theories help managers organize information and therefore are able to approach the problems systematically. Without theories, all managers will have ideas or creations which would not be useful in today's complex and dynamic organizations. However , there is no universally accepted and agreed theory of management that managers can apply in all situations.

Theories/ Approaches of Schools of Management Thought

Introduction

The management school of thought refers to the theories of ideas that were developed in a historical sequence by the early management writers. The systematic development of management thinking dates from the nineteenth century with the emergence of large industrial organizations and arising problems associated with their structure and management.

Types of Theories of Schools of Management

1.Scientific Theory

The primary concern of scientific management was to increase productivity through greater efficiency in production and increased pay for workers through the application of scientific methods.

Scientific management is based on the ideas of economic rationality, efficiency, individualism and scientific analysis of work. Fredrick W. Taylor acknowledged as the father of scientific management, was a major contributor to the approach. Some of his principles usually summarized include:-

i.   The development of true science for each person's work

ii.   The scientific selection, training and development of the workers

iii.   Improvement of methods of work to reduce workers' fatigue

iv.   Development of different accurate methods of paying workers

v.   Co- operation with the workers to ensure work is carried out in prescribed way

vi.   Minimization of physical effort

vii.   Elimination of duplication of work

Scientific Theory Limitations:-

i.　　　Workers are treated like machines i.e. are not allowed to think on their own

ii. Management is more concerned of work out put than welfare of workers

iii. Setting of strict work deadlines

iv. Limiting work processes with objective of causing it to become routine

2. Classical Theory

The classical writers thought of the organization in forms of its purpose and formal structure. They placed a lot of emphasis on planning work, the technical equipment of the organization, principles of management and the assumption of rational and logical behaviour. Writers Mooney and Reiley set out a number of principles which relate to all types of organization.

i.　　　The principle of coordination:- the need to act together with unity of action, the exercise of authority and the need for discipline

ii.　　　The scalar principle:- the hierarchy of organization, the grading of duties and the process of delegation

iii.　　　The functional principle:- specialization and distinction between different kinds of duties

Division of work: Clear definition of duties and responsibilities and maintaining specialization and co- ordination was given attention with emphasis on hierarchy of management and formal organization relationship.

The fundamental proposition is that people should be selected and trained to suit the organization needs but not to be structured to fit the human needs particularly individual needs.

Classical theory emphasized on formal rules, specialization, clear division of labor and the achievement of high efficiency through the analysis of work and attaching little importance to personal and social needs of the people operating in the organization.

Contributions of Classical School

Nevertheless, although regarded as an outdated approach, it focuses on important factors in organization and management. Through the division of labour, management by exception and specialization, some companies for example Export Processing Zone embrace these ideologies at the operational level. Here work is done in controlled conditions involving the most efficient working methods in order to achieve optimum organizational output.

The classical school does not take sufficient account of personality factors. It ignores the employees welfare and creates an organization structure in which people can exercise only a limited control over their work environment. Formal and hierarchical interpersonal relationships within organization are out of touch with the more liberal and democratic attitudes towards work relations today.

Classical approaches are rigid and the structures they imply are not usually capable of accommodating rapid, technical, environmental and other changes experienced in the modern world. Classical approach was suitable for the nineteenth and early twentieth century when technologies and organizational hierarchies were more precise. Owing to the complex and fast changing business world, this approach may not be suitable.

Constant repetition of simple movements dehumanizes work and in the long run, production reduces especially in the modern world when workers expectations and ambitions are very high.

Industrial efficiency together with the loss of individual control over working practices and procedures implied by the scientific approach naturally lead in unemployment which, is one of the biggest challenges facing developing countries

This approach was ideal when mass production was widely used in the manufacturing industries and it fitted well with the technology of that time. Current technical, economic and social circumstances are so completely different from those prevailing in the early years that the application of the approach may no longer be appropriate.

These logically determined and rational theories form the basis from which today's management practices thrive. Managers use these practices to effectively and efficiently attain organizational goals. Large organizations for example Bamburi, Unilever, East African Breweries among many other companies in Kenya engage the aspects of planning, organizing, controlling and leading as a regular practice in their daily operations.

Industrial undertakings saw the provision of administrative mechanism suitable for large organizations, with the separation of certain activities like technical (production, manufacture, adaptation); commercial (buying, selling, exchange);financial (search for optimal use of capital) security (protection of property and persons) accounting (stocktaking, balance sheets, costs, statistics) and managerial (forecasting, planning ,organizing, directing, controlling and coordination). These mechanisms have stood the test of time and are commonly used for efficient and effective management of modern large organizations.

This approach laid a firm foundation for subsequent study of the efficiency of working methods and organizations that are widely adopted in the modern organizations. Management studies is said to have transformed with the time taking into consideration different views previously ignored to what is widely acceptable today where managers draw their references for ideal management.

With emphasis on the role target setting and the need for logically determined standards, mass production was enhanced and improved quality achieved. Many organizations achieve their goals by setting targets and deadlines to their employees in order to survive in the market. A good example is the Japanese car manufacture Toyota where employees' production capacities are stretched to attain maximum productivity.

By insisting on the existence of general principles of management, classical approach complimented the need for management training in order to empower employees with abilities needed to apply these principles to enhance work performance; job training is one aspect that is still practiced by many companies to nurture worker skills for work improvement.

3. Behavioural Theory /Human Relations

Whereas the classical school sought to increase production by rationalization of the work organization, the human relations school dealt with ideas of increasing production by humanizing the work organization. The human relations school asserts that workplace behavior is determined mainly by the organizational setting in which it occurs. Thus social factors are regarded as influencing the actions and attitudes of workers at least as powerfully as incentive schemes and physical working conditions, leadership styles, interpersonal and organizational communications, employee morale, group norms and job satisfaction are deemed especially important.

The fundamental propositions of the human relations include;-

I. The amount of work a person does depends not so much on physical strength or mental abilities and not even on the physical conditions in which tasks are performed, rather it depends on the social conditions surrounding the work. Non economical rewards can motivate workers more than high wages; feeling of happiness and security often results from factors independent of pay

ii. Specialization and the division of labour might not be efficient. Giving workers a wider variety of tasks- some of which require the exercise of initiative and discretion – can stimulate employees interest in their work to the point where productivity actually increases

iii. Individuals perceive themselves as members of groups. Norms of behaviour emanate from standards set by the group to which workers belong and not from standards imposed by management.

Contributions

The human relations school recognizes clearly the role and importance of interpersonal relations at work. In the world today, interpersonal relations in group relations in group behaviour is given a lot of attention especially in the work place since it is through these groups that individuals associate with, that influence workers motivation. Employees generally view the organizations they work for through the values and attitudes of their colleagues. Good working relations motivate employees to perform better at their jobs.

People go to work to satisfy a wide range of needs and not only for monetary rewards. Much as employees would expect to be paid for their work, they have many other needs like appreciation from their managers or employers. Successful managers give attention to these needs in order to get the best performance from the workers.

It criticized the assumption that society consists of groups of greedy individuals each attempting selfishly to maximize their personal self interest. With the arrest of this view, managers and workers relationship improved and with the change in attitude today we see better working conditions.

This approach showcased how social and technical systems interrelate. The importance of the informal organization which will always be present within the formal structure saw the recognition of how the social conditions influenced the organizations and how the organizations influenced their workers.

It highlighted links between job satisfaction and productivity. Involving workers in more challenging duties and decisions that affect their working lives is essential for effective management. Employers who encourage workers participation through joint consultation, suggestion schemes etc tend to achieve better output because workers tend to be highly motivated. Practitioners in modern management practices support the involvement of worker representatives in management decisions on the grounds that it develops social cohesion, highlights the principle of fair treatment for labour and distributes power to more people in business organization.

Limitations

However, depending on the current environmental circumstances, organizational needs and objectives tend to vary a great deal. As much as ideological concerns for personal development and individual rights are laudable objectives, they ignore the existence of conflicts of interest within, for example, frustrations and disagreements between management and workers.

It does not take full potential of the effects of the organizational structure on the individual with a lot of emphasis placed on the employees and how they influence the organization. This approach tends to downplay the role of the organizational structure on the employees.

The human relations school views organizations as closed systems and ignore political, economic and other environmental forces, since organization needs and objectives vary enormously depending on the current environmental circumstances, it may not be suitable in the world where environmental circumstances are very dynamic.

The labour unions play a big role on the influence of employee's attitude and behaviour today since this approach did not highlight on the influence of labour unions on the employee attitude and behaviour. Conflicts may be inevitable.

Motivation, the employees desire to participate in decision making and their occupation, self awareness is highly overrated since not everyone wants to control their work. In fact many workers have little idea of what they actually expect or desire from employment experience and often seek direction from higher level of authority

Attention is focused on the influence of small groups while neglecting the effects of the wider social structures within which groups exist. For example by encouraging employees participation in areas of serious decision making, this could lead to devastating effects on the organization since the decision making process becomes extremely slow.

4. The System Theory

The classical approach emphasizes on the technical requirements of the organization and its need 'organizations without people', the human relations approach emphasized on the psychological and social aspects and the consideration of human needs.

The systems approach attempts to reconcile other approaches and the work of other writers of the management. Attention is focused on the total world organization and the interrelations of structure, behaviour and the range of variables within the organization. This approach can be constructed with a view of the organization as separate parts. The systems approach encourages managers to view the organization both as a whole and as part of larger environment. The idea is that any part of an organization's activities affects all other parts

There are two types of systems.

i) A closed system is one that is independent of its environment, determines its own destiny and controls its own internal relationships. The continuing existence of a closed system does not depend on it entering transaction with the outside world. The other type is ii)The open system, which is in continuous contact with their environment and the boundaries of such systems are neither rigid nor easily defined. Open systems have the following characteristics

.   They must enter transactions with their environment e.g. a firm must recruit workers and persuade customers to purchase its goods

.   They need to be able to adapt to external change

.   They transform inputs obtained from the environment into outputs returned to the environment e.g. a firm transforms labour, materials and capita-goods and services.

Contributions

The system approach is considerate of all organizations activities since it integrates the other approaches thus making it better and more applicable in the modern world. Since it is holistic, many diverse organizations adapt these viewpoints.

Since it incorporates both the classical school and human relations school which are transformed as inputs (raw materials and human resources) into outputs (products or consumer services) this interrelationship enables organizations to trace the effects of one element of the system through the changes in the other.

Factors that affect output (production) such as inputs (human resources and the firm's components) can be monitored to give the optimum production. The relationship between inputs and outputs are examined.

A system is a set of interrelated components that work together to achieve a common goal. This ideology has enabled models depicting causes and effects within a particular system to be constructed for example the computer.

Limitations

Systems theory highlights very few tangible propositions about how managers should behave. Systems theory is abstract and lacks prompt discernible applications

Organization systems consist of and are run by people thus interpersonal relations might be more important than particular input –output structures and organizational forms which they control.

Since various components are taken into consideration to enhance production, the systems theory has little to say about the causes of motivation to work hard within various types of systems

The boundaries of systems might change according to circumstances and over time, for example due to changing patterns of distribution.

Different members of the same system have entirely different structures and aims thus creating conflicts.

Certain advocates of the systems approach have used it to justify centralization of administrative procedures in entirely inappropriate circumstances. The tendency to enforce centralization follows the adoption of holistic perspective causing the desire to concentrate decisions at the top of the organization.

Organizational relationships are often highly complex. In these cases the application of the systems approach might naively simplify what is an enormously complicated problem. There is a vast range of variables potentially relevant to organizational performance so that the specialization of just a few inputs and constraints is bound to be arbitrary to some degree.

Systems theory cannot by of itself explain organizational behaviour without taking other considerations into account.

It takes the actions of a single individual to instantly transform the nature of a system.

5. The Contingency Theory

The contingency approach, which can be seen as an extension of the systems approach, highlights possible means of differentiating among alternative forms of organization structures and systems of management. There is no one optimum state. For example, the structure of the organization and its success are dependent, that is contingent upon, the nature of tasks which it is designed to deal and the nature of environmental influences.

The most appropriate structure and systems of management is therefore dependent upon the contingencies of the situation of each particular organization. The contingency approach implies that the organization theory should not seek to suggest the best way to structure or manage organization but should provide insights into situational and contextual factors which influence management decisions.

The adoption of contingency approach releases managers from the rigid structures imposed by other schools. Managers simply tailor their behavior to the needs of various situations. Certainly it offers some valuable insights for the practicing managers. Not all factors affecting leadership styles are in harmony with each other in real life situations. Some factors in a situation may favour a people-oriented styles and others a task-oriented style. Contingency thinking can help the manager find systematic ways to handle even the most complicated situations.

The application of modern contingency theory can help contribute to a more successful organization, economic pressures and rapid developments in information technology necessitating the review of structural design.

If contingency approach is to be useful in guiding organization design, it should not treat every situation as unique. Thus the modern theory uses limited number of contingencies to help explain structural differences between organizations.

Contingency thinking forces the manager to abandon the pursuit of single best approach. The best approach may be determined only after a careful analysis of the task and the people involved.

Limitations

However, the contingency approach experiences certain problems. A manager who behaves in this manner may appear insincere and inconsistent to colleagues and particularly subordinates. One approach is adopted today and possibly an entirely different approach tomorrow , according to circumstances. Subordinates and others never know what to expect from the manager. Advocates of the contingency approach might object to this assertion on the grounds that management role is to allocate different managers to the roles and situations for which they are best suited. In practice, however, most managers will necessarily experience a variety of situations and need to occupy several roles in the course of their work.

Contingency models of organization fail to give sufficient emphasis to unanticipated consequences of planned change, for example, the effects of the introduction of new technology on the internal working of the organization of social interactions among groups of people engaged in certain activities.

Changes in structure tend to lag behind situational change therefore; there is a degree of luck about whether at any moment in time there is a good fit between and prevailing contingency factors.

The common view in contingency theory is that the match among components of the organization and situation variables related to maximizing organizational performance. However it is impossible to get a single criterion for the appropriateness of the fit among various features of organization and improve performance.

The individual manager may not be sufficiently skilled or mature to be able to change his or her approach from one situation to the next, especially if the manager has not been trained in the techniques of contingency management.

It may be entirely appropriate to apply certain basic principles regardless of circumstances, particularly where professional ethics and moral issues are concerned.

Chapter 1/5: MANAGERIAL ROLES

Introduction

The work of a manager is multi-disciplinary. Managers perform many functions such as forecasting, planning, organizing, directing, controlling and coordination.

To meet the many demands of performing their functions, managers assume multiple roles.

Definition of a role

A role is an organized set of objectives (Henry Mintzberg, 1973).

Role of Managers:-

i.	Figure head	vi.	Spokesperson
ii.	Leader	vii.	Entrepreneur

iii.	Liaison	viii.	Disturbance handler
iv.	Monitor	ix.	Resource allocator
v.	Disseminator	x.	Negotiator

Divisions of managerial roles with specific roles:-

1.Interpersonal Roles

i.   Figure head

ii.   Leader

iii.   Liaison

2. Informational Roles

i.   Monitor

ii.   Disseminator

iii.   Spokesperson

3. Decisions Roles

i.   Entrepreneur

ii.   Disturbance handler

iii.   Resource allocator

iv.   Negotiator

Elaboration of divisions of roles of managers:-

1. Interpersonal Roles

The three interpersonal roles are primarily concerned with interpersonal relationships. In the figure head role, the manager represents the organization in all matters formality.

The top level management represents the company legally and socially to those outside the organization.

The supervisor represents the work group to higher management and higher management to the work group.

In the liaison role, the manager interacts with peers and people outside the organization. The top level manager uses the liaison role to gain favours and information while the supervisor uses it to maintain the routine flow of work. The leader role defines the relationship between the manager and employees.

2. Informational Roles

The direct relationship with people in the interpersonal roles place the manager in a unique position to get information, thus, the three informational roles are primarily concerned with the information aspects of management work.

In the monitor role, the manager receives and collects information.

In the role of disseminator, the manager transmits special information into the organization.

The top level manager receives and transmits more information from people outside the organization than the supervisor.

In the role of spokesperson, the manager disseminates the organization's information into the environment. Thus, the top level manager is seen as an industry expert, while the supervisor is seen as a unit or departmental expert.

3. Decisional Roles

The unique access to information places the manager at the centre of organization decision making.

There are four decision roles. In the entrepreneur role, the manager initiates change. In the disturbance handler role, the manager deals with threats to the organization, the manager chooses where the organization will expand its efforts.

In the negotiators role, the manager negotiates on behalf of the organization. The top level manager makes the decisions about the organization as a whole, while the supervisor makes decisions about his or her particular work unit.

The supervisor performs these managerial roles but with different emphasis than higher managers. Supervisory management is more focused and short term in outlook. Thus, the figurehead role becomes less significant and the disturbance handler and negotiator roles increase in importance for the supervisor

Since leadership permeates all activities, the leader role is among important of all roles at all levels of management.

CHAPTER TWO

Chapter 2/1: THE WRITERS OF THE

HISTORY OF MANAGEMENT THINKING

Introduction

The writers of the history of management thinking wrote it with clear idea in their minds about what it was primarily trying to achieve.

The writers held the view that if certain principles of management or organization are put into practice, then the management will be more successful in ensuring that the objectives of the organization are achieved, in an efficient manner. Their aim was and still is , effectiveness and efficiency in the use of resources to achieve organizational goals.

THE WRITERS

1.   Fredrick W. Taylor (1856- 1917): Pioneered the scientific management movement. He argued that management should be based on well recognized, clearly defined and fixed principles, instead of depending on more or less clear ideas.

His purpose was to maximize efficiency and suggested that by offering workers more money for being efficient, both the workers and employers would benefit.

Taylor, further, reasoned that productivity would not be improved by the offer of more money alone; he argued that a radical change of attitudes, on the part of both management and workers was essential if his system was to be successful.

Taylor's famous four principles of scientific management

I. The development of a true science of work: all knowledge which had hitherto been kept in the heads of workers should be gathered and recorded by management.

ii. The scientific election and progressive development of workers: workers should be carefully trained and given jobs to which they are best suited.

iii. The bringing together of the science and the scientifically selected and trained workers: the application of techniques to decide what should be done, using workers who are properly trained and willing to maximize output, should result in maximum productivity.

iv. The constant and intimate co operation between management and workers: the relations between employers and workers should be enhanced.

2. Henry Fayol (1841-1925): Henry Fayol, a French industrialist was another early writer associated with the classical school of management thought. He popularized the concept of universality of management principles. His principles allowed for flexibility in their application. Fayol argued that as managers rise up the scalar chain or organizational hierarchy, they need to show an increasing amount of managerial ability.

Fayol further argued that applying principles of management is a difficult art requiring intelligence and so on. He listed the following fourteen principles of good management

i. Division of work i.e. specialization: the aim of specialization is to produce more and obtain better results.

ii.   Authority and responsibility: He said that authority should be commensurate with responsibility. He further said that a good leader should encourage those around him to accept responsibility.

iii.   Discipline: he said that a fair system with penalties judiciously applied by worthy superiors can be of great strength to an organization.

iv.   Unity of command: for any action, a subordinate should receive orders from one superior only

v.   Unity of direction: there should be one head and one plan for each activity

vi.   The interest of one employee or group of employees : the interest of one employee or group of employees should not prevail over that of the general interest of the organization.

vii.   Remuneration: remuneration of personnel should be fair, satisfying both employer and employees alike.

viii.   Scalar chain (chain of command): Fayol said that a manager should observe every step in the chain i.e. he is not supposed to bypass any step, it has to be systematic.

ix.   Stability of tenure of personnel: employee careers should not be interrupted until an employee attains retirements age.

x.   Esprit decorps: good relations of employee should be strengthened

xi.   Initiative: it is essential to encourage and develop workers capacity up to the full.

xii.   Order: resources should be well coordinated such that they are at the required places at the right time

xiii.   Equity: managers should be kind and fair when dealing with subordinates

xiv.   Centralization: Fayol argued that workers cohesiveness should be strengthened by democratically enforcing principles of management

Fayol considered the main elements of management to be forecasting, planning, organizing, directing, controlling and coordination.

3. Mary Parker Follett (1868- 1933)

Mary Parker Follet saw management as a continuous process rather than a series of discrete events.

She suggested that in any industrial organization, everyone in the organization should have rational appreciation of what is required by the situation.

She further said that in giving orders, so as to unite all concerned, one person should not give orders to another person, but both should agree to take their orders from the situation. Mary further argued that it is not the duty of a manager to instruct a worker to obey a regulation: the duty of a manager should be to find out the reason of the failure to obey a regulation then give his managerial advice.

4. Elton Mayo

Elton Mayo was main contributor to behavioural School of management thought / human relations school.

Mayo was an academic based at Harvard University. Mayo was concerned by the way scientific school of management had dehumanized operations.

Elton Mayo conducted Hawthorne experiment to establish how high morale influences the productivity.

The experiment was conducted from 1927-36, during the world depression. The work of those involved in the research was to assemble electrical appliances.

At the beginning of the experiment, the productivity was high because guinea pigs were proud for being selected to participate in the experiment.

As the world depression worsened, the guinea pigs got worried, the conductors of the experiment noticed a decline in productivity and therefore stopped to treat guinea pigs as special i.e. they stopped to matter.

This experiment proves that a worker's level of productivity is influenced by his/her morale

5. Chester Barnard

Chester Bernard pioneered the systems approach to management theory. He took the view that an organization is a social system consisting of individuals who cooperate together within a formal framework.

His views briefly summarized are:

i.   Human beings are physically incapable of doing everything they need for themselves, therefore they must co operate with each other. Once co-operation begins out of physical needs, the concept of a cooperative is reinforced by psychological and social attitudes

ii.   Cooperation inevitably leads to the establishment of cooperative systems i.e organizations

iii.   Organizations can be formal (i.e consciously coordinated systems of human interactions, with a common purpose) or informal (i.e. social interactions without a conspicuous structure or common purpose)

iv.   Formal organization depends on:

. The ability of individuals in the system to communicate with each other

. A willingness to contribute towards group action

. Having a known conscious common purpose

v. Formal organizations must have;

. A system of dividing work into functional groupings, so that members can specialize.

. A system of incentives which will make group members contribute towards the common purpose

. A system of authority (or power) so that group members accept the decisions of supervisory management. A system of logical decision making

6. Max Weber (1863- 1920)

Max Weber spanned the same period of history as those early pioneers of management thought Fayol, Taylor et al. Unlike them, Weber was an academic – a sociologist and not a practising manager.

The observations and conclusions from his studies were first published in translation from the original Germany in 1947.

It was in 1947 when the term Bureaucracy came up. Bureaucracy has several definitions, for example, is a red tape i.e. excess of paperwork and rules leading to gross inefficiency.

Bureaucracy is 'officialdom' i.e. all the apparatus of central and local government are similar to red tape

Bureaucracy is also defined as an organizational form with certain dominant characteristics, such as a hierarchy of authority and a system of rules.

Weber's interest in organizations was from the point of view of their authority structures. He wanted to find out why people in organizations obeyed those in authority over them.

In his analysis of organizations, Weber identified three basic types of legitimate authority

i. Traditional: this is authority from traditional belief, for example, the first born of a monarch will become king or queen when the position falls vacant.

ii.   Charismatic: the authority will be bestowed on somebody due to his/her special talent recognized by others. For example a wise person will be obeyed by other people

iii.   Rational legal authority: the authority is bestowed on a person when the person is elected to a position.

The main features of a bureaucracy according to Max Weber are:

i.   A continuous organization of functions bound by rules

ii.   Specified spheres of competence, i.e. the specialization of work, the degree of allocated and the rules governing the exercise of authority.

iii.   A hierarchical arrangement of offices (jobs), i.e. where one level of jobs is controlled by next higher level.

iv.   Appointment to offices are made on grounds of technical competence

v.   The separation of officials from the ownership of the organization.

vi.   Official positions exist in their own right and job holders have no right to a particular position.

vii.   Rules, decisions and actions are formulated and recorded in writing.

The above features of bureaucratic organization enable the authority of offices subject to published rules and practices.

Contributions of bureaucracy:-

i.   The definition of responsibilities and duties of each position within the hierarchy derives from the overall objectives of the organization and there is no room for subversion of those objectives.

ii.   Work is highly regulated in that, every eventuality is covered by the laid down rules and procedures

iii.   All tasks are covered by the hierarchy of suspension which ensures the desired level of performance.

iv.   The existence of tight job descriptions and person specifications means that staff have specific skills and abilities related directly to the tasks to be performed.

v.   The bureaucratic form strongly supports the application of rules and regulations which create a feeling of certainty that provides a stress free workplace.

vi.   Security of employment and impersonality of work practices and procedures encourage faithful performance of duties, confidence in the system and opportunities within a regularized promotion system which removes office competition.

Limitations of bureaucracy:-

i.   Impersonality can ensure a common level of treatment and lack of responsiveness to individual incidents.

ii.   Relationships are inhibited, meaning that social and ego needs are unsatisfied

iii.   Individual circumstances vary infinitely and trying to apply rigid rules can mean inefficiency , even injustice, in the non – standard case

iv.   Initiative may be stifled as rules become ends in themselves

v.   Bureaucratic rules/ procedures can cause a lack of flexibility or adaption to changing circumstances.

vi.   There can be a lack of attention to the informal organization and the development of groups and their goals.

vii.   Handling problems in a standard fashion instead of using their own initiative does not satisfy most workers' needs.

viii.   Environments are becoming more dynamic and prone to change. There is therefore need for dynamic organization and relationships in a changing environment.

Chapter 2/2: Management by Objectives (MbO)

Introduction

Management by objectives concept was introduced by Peter Drucker in 1954. The approach was improved by Douglas McGregor who advocated its use as a preferred means of goal setting, appraisal of managerial performance and self assessment. The system of management by objectives has been adopted in a wide range of organizational setting, in the public as well as the private sector.

Definition of management by objectives

Management by objectives is a process whereby the superior and subordinate managers of an organization jointly identify its common goals and define each individual's major areas of responsibility in terms of the results expected of him and use these measures as guides for operating the unit and assessing the contribution of each of its members (Ordione).

The cycle of MbO activities:-

MbO involves a continuous cycle of interrelated activities

I. The clarification of organizational goals and objectives: These should be communicated clearly to, and understood fully by, all members of staff.

ii. Review of organizational structure: the need is for a flexible structure and systems of management which make for effective communications, quick decision making and timely feedback information.

iii. Participation with subordinates in order to gain their willing acceptance of objectives and targets, key result area and standards and measurement of performance.

iv. Agreement on performance improvement plans which will enable subordinates to make the optimum contribution to a) meeting their own objectives and targets; b) improved organizational performance.

v. Establishment of an effective monitoring review system for appraisal of progress and performance, including self checking and evaluation.

vi. Undertaking any necessary revision to/or restatement of subordinates objectives and targets

vii. Review of organizational performance against stated goals and objectives

Diagram

Requirements of a successful MbO programme:-

i.   The commitment and active support of top management.

ii.   Specialist advice on implementation of the system and a thorough understanding by all the staff concerned.

iii.   Careful attention to the setting of key tasks, target figures and performance standards.

iv.   Objectives which are profitable to the organization clearly defined, realistically attainable and capable of measurement.

v.   Genuine participation by staff in agreeing to objectives and targets.

vi.   The right spirit and interest from staff concerned and effective teamwork.

vii.   Avoidance of excessive paperwork and forms.

viii.   Maintaining the impetus of the system.

Advantages of MbO are:-

i.   Concentrates attention on main areas where it is important for the organization to be effective.

ii.   Identifies problem areas in progress towards achievement of objectives.

iii.   Improves management control information and performance standards.

iv.   Leads to a sound organization structure, clarifies responsibilities, aids delegation and co ordination.

v.   Identifies where changes are needed and seeks continual improvement in results.

vi.   Aids management succession planning.

vii.   Identifies training needs, provides an environment which encourages personal growth and self discipline.

viii.   Improves appraisal systems and provides a more equitable procedure for determining rewards and promotional plans.

ix.   Improves communications and interpersonal relationships.

x.   Encourages motivation to improve individual performance.

Disadvantages of MbO:-

i.   It is not always easy to set specific targets or figures for certain more senior jobs.

ii.   There is a potential danger that where objectives and targets are more difficult to specify and measure in precise terms, are neglected.

iii.   Most managers place greater emphasis on objectives which are more easily monitored.

iv.   MbO appears to have suffered some decline in popularity

v.   Developing Mbo programme is costly.

vi.   The time spent in developing an MbO programme is high.

vii.   MbO programme are very flexible i.e. they are frequently redrawn to match changes in the organization.

CHAPTER THREE

MANAGEMENT AND ORGANIZATIONS

Management environment

Introduction

There are many ways of looking at organizations. One approach, taken by systems theorists is that an organization is a social system or socio-technical system. A system may be defined as a collection of parts into a complex unity, or as organized complexity. A social system is, therefore, a grouping of many individual people in to a unified body; and a socio- technical system is a co-operative social system in which human attitudes and behavior are influenced by the technology of work (i.e machines and work methods).

In system theory, a distinction is made between;-

i.   Closed systems, i.e. systems which are cut off from their environment and do not interact with their environment.

ii.   Open system i.e. systems whose operations are influenced by their environment and which in turn will also have some influence on their environment. All social organizations such as business organizations are open system.

An organization is a unified, complex system: it has identity and has boundaries which divide it from its environment. For example, a bank might be identified as a grouping of shareholders, directors, employees and physical assets. Suppliers, competitors and customers would then be regarded as part of the environment of the system. However, employees of the company may also be members of a trade union, their church, a political party, local government, a board of school governors etc. therefore individuals belong to several organizations at the same time. Similarly, an employee may himself have a bank account and make use of the services offered by his company; he would then be a customer as well as a member of the organization.

An organization may have boundaries, but their boundaries are neither rigid nor impenetratable.

Three Aspects Of Environment Influence

Koontz, O'Donnell and Weihrich identified three ways in which the environment is related to an organization.

i.   The organization imports resources from the environment. Raw materials, plant, equipment and other fixed assets are obtained from outside suppliers. Employees are recruited from an external pool of labour etc.

ii.   There are many different groups in the environment or connected in some way with the environment, and each of these groups may have some rights or claims with regard to the activities of the organization. These groups include customers, employees (who as previously described, are members of several organizations at the time). The government, the general public, suppliers and share holders.

iii.   The environment provides opportunities which an organization can exploit e.g. for a company new market and for a hospital, new medical discoveries and threats which endanger the organization's survival (e.g. for a company, competitors actions, the threat of restrictive government legislation, political unrest etc.). Such opportunities and threats may be commercial, political, technological, economic, social or ethical.

The three types of relationship are complementary, and all of them exists Koontz, O'Donnell and Weihrich wrote:

'Every time managers plan, they take into account the needs and desires of members of society outside the organization, as well as needs for material and human resources, technology and other requirements in the external environment. They do likewise to some degree with almost every other kind of managerial activity. All managers, whether they operate in business, a government agency, a church, a charitable foundation or a unity, must in varying degrees, take into account the elements and forces of their external environment. While they may be able to do little or nothing to change these forces, they have no alternative but to respond to them'.

Types of external and internal environmental forces

Management operations in organizations are influenced by;

1. External forces

External forces in organizations include;-

i.   Competitors: Competitors are a threat in management operations. Management is forced to respond to the activities of the competitors e.g. when competitors reduce price, the management has to improve its operations.

ii.   Customers: Management is forced to respond to the demands of the customers so that they continue buying the organizations' products or services.

iii.   The government: The management is forced to respond positively to the government requirements especially, they have to pay the demanded tax.

iv.   Political environment: Management has to respond to the new social pressures and views of the political party in power.

v.   Legal environment: Management is forced to respond to legal controls affecting the organization, such as to manage their employees according to the requirements of employment act and a wide range of other legislation and case law.

vi.   The state organized environment: The government owns many organizations, such as state education, the police, National Health Service and civil service departments etc. Management is forced to respond to the requirements of government organizations.

vii.   The technological environment: Technology refers to the ways of getting things done i.e. to scientific inventions and developments and also methods of working. Management is forced to introduce new technology so as to improve its efficiency.

viii. The social environment: The social environment consists of the customs, attitudes, beliefs and education of society as a whole or of different groups in society. Management is forced to respond to employees, customs, beliefs and attitudes so as to maintain good relations.

ix.   The ethical environment: The ethical environment of organizations refers to justice, respect for the law and moral code. The conduct of an organization, its management and employees will be measured against ethical standards by the customers, suppliers and other members of the public with whom they deal.

2. Internal forces

Internal environment forces in organization include:

I. Policies: Management operation will be affected by the formulated policies.

ii. Rules: Rules influence the operations of the management

iii. Finance: Limited funds will affect the operations of the management i.e. it will be unable to hire qualified personnel

iv. Trade unions: The activities of the trade union will influence the decision of the management

v. Management skill: Limited skills of management will cause management to postpone an idea or a project

vi. Plans: Predetermined plans will limit on what an organization can or cannot do.

vii. Management philosophy: Workers behaviour in the working place will be influenced by the set philosophy of the management.

viii. Informal groups: Activities of informal group members will affect positively or negatively activities of management.

Chapter 3/2: ORGANIZATIONAL GOALS AND OBJECTIVES OF BUSINESS

ORGANIZATION

Introduction

All organizations have some functions to perform, some contributions to make to the environment of which they are part. The function off business organization may be seen, for example, as the creation and/ or supply of goods and services.

In addition to performing some functions, all organizations also have some incentive for their existence, and for their operations. The goals of an organization are the reason for its existence. The activities of the organization are directed to the attainment of its goals.

Definition

A goal is a future expectation, some desired future state.

The concept of organizational goals

The concept of organizational goals is more specific than that of the functions of an organization.

The goals of an organization will determine the nature of its inputs and outputs, the series of activities through which the outputs are achieved and interactions with its external environment.

The extent to which an organization is successful in attaining its goals is a basis for the evaluation of organizational performance and effectiveness.

The concept of organizational goals is ambiguous. Goals may be expressed very simply in the case of business organizations, for example, to make a profit or to increase productivity. Such broadly based goals might be taken for granted and they tell little about the emphasis placed on the various activities of the organization in meeting its goals. In any case, profit might more correctly be interpreted as a reward to the shareholders or providers of capital and a means of ensuring continued existence of the organization and maintaining its growth and development.

Informal goals and formal goals

Members of the organization have different and often conflicting goals. As a result the goals which the organization actually pursues (informal goals) may be distinguished from the officially stated goals. (Formal goals) which are set out in broad terms and the reasons for the purpose of the organization.

Incompatibility of goals

If organizational goals and personal goals are pulling in different directions, conflict will arise and performance is likely to suffer.

An organization will be more effective when personal goals are compatible with organizational goals.

Management has a responsibility to clarify organizational goals and to attempt to integrate personal goals (including their own) with the overall objectives of the organization. Only when organizational goals are shared by all members of the organization, will complete integration be achieved.

Management should endeavour, therefore to structure the organization so that people may realize their own (personal) goals by helping the organization to satisfy its goals.

One attempt at integrating organizational goals with the needs of the individual members of the organization is provided by the approach of Management by Objectives.

Organization ideologies and principles

The goals of the organization may be pursued in accordance with an underlying ideology or philosophy, based on beliefs, values and attitudes.

This ideology determines the culture of the organization and provides a set of principles which govern the overall conduct of the organization's operations, codes of behaviour, the management of people and its dealings with other organizations.

Important principles in business

i.   Perhaps the most important of all is a policy of good human relations with all concerned in an with the operation- employees, customers and suppliers.

ii.   To offer customers goods and services which they want and which should be of a high quality and good value

iii.   To work closely with suppliers and encourage them to use the most modern and efficient techniques of production and quality control dictated by the latest discoveries in science and technology.

iv.   To simplify operating procedures so that the business is carried out in an efficient manner

v.   To ensure that those in management are not isolated or in watertight compartments and that while in an individual's responsibility (other than the chief executive's) may be limited to a particular area or areas he or she should have general knowledge of the operation as a whole.

vi.   Never forget the importance of satisfying the customers.

vii.   To seek wherever possible a source in the nation.

Organizational objectives and policy

In accordance with its ideology or philosophy, the goals of the organization are translated into objectives and policy.

Terminology and use of two terms varies but objectives are seen here as the "what" and policy as the "how" "where" and "when" the means that follow the objectives.

Objectives set out more specifically the goals of the organization, the aims to be achieved and the desired end results.

Policy is developed within the framework of objectives. It provides the basis for decision making and the course decision making and the action to follow in order to achieve objectives.

The relationship between the organization, its objectives and management is illustrated by Henry Fayol who stated that one of the managerial duties of an organization is to see that the human and material resources in organization is consistent with the objectives, resources and requirements of the concern.

The establishment of objectives and policy is therefore an integral part of the process of management and a necessary function in every organization.

A systematic view of goals and objectives

The objectives of an organization are related to the input conversion- output cycle. In order to achieve its objectives and satisfy its goals, the organization takes inputs from the environment through a series of activities, transforms or converts these inputs into outputs and return to the environment as inputs to other systems.

The organization operates within a dynamic setting and success in achieving its goals will be influenced by a multiplicity of interactions with the environment

What the type of organization, there is need for line of direction through the establishment of objectives and determination of policy. Objectives and policy form a basis for the process of management.

Objectives

The choice of objectives is an essential part of the decision making process involving future courses of action. Objectives may be set out either in general terms or in more specific terms.

General objectives are determined by top management and specific objectives are formulated within the scope of general objectives and usually have more defined areas of application and time limits.

Objectives may be just implicit but the formal, explicit definition of objectives will help highlight the activities which the organization needs to undertake and the comparative importance of its various functions. An explicit statement of objectives may assist communications and reduce misunderstandings and provide more meaningful criteria for evaluation organizational performance. However objectives should be stated n such a way that they detract from the recognition of possible new opportunities, potential danger areas, the initiative of staff or the need for innovation or change.

Policy guideline

A policy is a guideline for organizational action and the implementation of goals and objectives. Policy is translated into rules, plans and procedures; it relates to all activities of the organization, and to all levels of the organization.

Clearly stated policy can help reinforce the main functions of the organization, make for consistency and reduce dependency on the actions of individual managers.

Policy clarifies the roles and responsibilities of managers and other members of staff and provides guidelines for managerial behaviour.

Securing agreement to a new revised policy can help overcome reliance on outdated practices and aid the introduction of organization change.

Policy provides guiding principles for areas of decision making and delegation. For example, specific decision making relating to personnel policy could include:

i.   To give priority to promotion form the within the organization.

ii.   To enforce retirement at government pensionable age.

iii.   Whenever possible to employ only graduate or professionally qualified managers and accountants.

iv.   To permit line managers in consultation with the human resource to appoint staff upto a given salary/ wage level.

Some policy decisions are directly influenced by external factors, for example government legislation on equal opportunities.

Objectives of Business Organization

In order to be successful, the primary objectives of the business organization may be seen as:

- To continue in existence, that is to survive

- To maintain growth and development, and

- To make profit

All three objectives are closely linked and it is a matter of debate whether the organization survives and develops in order to provide a profit, or makes a profit by which it can survive and develop.

 If the survival is accepted as the ultimate objective of the business organization, then this involves the need for a steady and continuous profit.

Organizations must be prepared to accept the possibility of a reduction in short term profitability in order for future investments.

The profit goal is achieved through the process of management and the combined efforts of members of the organization.

In practice, there are many other considerations and motivations which affect the desire for the greatest profit or maximum economic efficiency and the accompanying assumption which underlie the economic theory of the organization (see the diagram below)

diagram

CHAPTER FOUR

MANAGEMENT IN PRACTICE

Chapter 4/1: STRATEGIC MANAGEMENT

Introduction

Managing activities internal to the company is only part of the modern executive's responsibilities. The modern executive also responds to the challenges posed by the company's immediate and remote external environment. The immediate external environment includes competitors, suppliers, increasingly scarce resources, government regulations and customers whose preferences often shift inexplicably.

The remote external environment comprises of economic and social conditions, political priorities, and a technological development, all of which must be anticipated, monitored, assessed and incorporated into the executive's decision making.

To deal effectively with everything that affects the growth and profitability of a company, executives employ management processes that they feel will position it optimally in its competitive environment by maximizing anticipation of environmental changes and of unexpected internal and competitive demands

Definition

Strategic management is defined as the set of decisions and actions that result in the formulation and implementation of plans designed to achieve a company's objectives.

Strategic thinking

Strategizing is about taking stock of where the organization is today and where it ought to be within a reasonable timescale (say five years). It is about deciding how to get there – the need for objectives and plans for bridging the gap between the present position and the desired future.

Strategic thinking in business is largely a matter of common sense, some knowledge, training and considerable experience. A question of intuition i.e. a feeling that some situation exists or is likely to exist when one has insufficient evidence for drawing that conclusion by logical reasoning, the ability to draw conclusions and take the corrective action.

The questions for consideration by the manager include:

i.   What business are we in and what business should we be in?

ii.   What advantages do we have compared with our leading competitors?

iii.   What are our major opportunities for growth and increased profitability?

iv.   What are threats and our continued survival and development?

Strategic planning process:-

i.   Plan to plan i.e. first think of a set of procedures to be followed. A plan focused on the execution of the planning process must be made

ii.   Situation audit: the situation audit embraces the crucial data gathering and analytical activities that should be undertaken early in the planning process.

iii.   Forecasts: forecast data are an essential part of the situation audit mainly projecting the economic factors that have an impact on the enterprise.

iv.   Inclusion of external interests: consider the needs of stock holders, customers, suppliers, creditors, local community, special interest groups etc.

v.   Expectations of major internal interests: the top management and other employees have a lot to say regarding strategy.

Modes of strategy formulation

Strategy may be formulated in a variety of ways. Henry Mintzberg has set forth some of the following general modes of organizational strategy formulation.

i.   Entrepreneurial

Here strategy is formulated by one person usually the owner- manager (entrepreneur). This mode is characterized by bold risk taking decision based primarily on intuition and personal preferences. This mode is found most in small businesses.

ii.   Planning mode

Here the central focus is on formal planning process, which provides a framework for making strategic decisions

SWOT Analysis

A traditional approach to internal analysis

SWOT is an acronym for the internal strength and weakness of a firm and the environmental opportunities and threats facing the firm. SWOT analysis is a historical popular technique through which managers create a quick overview of company's strategic situation.

It is based on assumption that an effective strategy derives from a sound fit between a firm's internal resources (strengths and weaknesses) and its external situation (opportunities and threats)

An example of a brief SWOT analysis based on a typical Kenya's supermarket chain:-

STRENGTHS

i.   Wide spread coverage.

ii.   Light and airly stores.

iii.   Ample parking.

iv.   Attractive new development.

v.   Wide range of goods.

vi.   Instore services (eg pharmacy/post office).

vii.   Competitive pricing on many products.

viii.   Convenient locations.

ix.   Petrol station.

x.   Excellent cash flow.

xi.   Provision of local bus services (free).

WEAKNESSES

i.   Substantial reliance on part time employees.

ii.   Overcrowding of stores at peak times.

iii.   Reliance on regular transport of products from regional cold stores.

iv.   Profitability at risk from price reductions on certain key goods.

OPPORTUNITIES

i.   Attract bank/building society cash points

ii.   Encourage use of bottle banks

iii.   Provide space for mobile library

iv.   Community projects (e.g. computers for schools)

v.   Open new stores in viable locations

vi.   Source new suppliers (home/overseas)

THREATS

i.   Local competition from other major supermarkets chains.

ii.   Price cutting by competitors.

iii.   Failure to obtain planning permission for new developments.

Limitations of SWOT Analysis

A SWOT analysis can over emphasize internal strengths and downplay external threats; strategists in every company have to remain vigilant against building strategies around what the firm does well now (its strength) without due considerations of the external environment's impact on those strengths.

A SWOT analysis can be static and can risk ignoring changing circumstances. A frequent admonition about the downfall of planning processes says that plans are onetime events to be complete, typed and relegated to their spot on a manager's shelf while he/she goes about the actual work on the firm so it is not surprising that critics of SWOT analysis, with good reason, is in that it is a onetime view of a changing, or moving situation.

Bottom line: SWOT analysis, along with most planning techniques, must avoid being static and ignoring change

A SWOT analysis can overemphasize a single strength or element of strategy.

Bottom line: strategies should never rely one's strength because unforeseen circumstances can occur that negatively affect the outcome.

Strength is not necessarily a source of competitive advantage.

Three levels of strategy

i.   Corporate level

Composed principally of:-

- Board of directors

- The chief executive

- Administrative officers

Functions:-

- Responsible for firm's financial performance

- Achievement of non financial goals such as enhancing the firm's image and fulfilling its social responsibilities.

- Set objectives

- Formulate strategies that span the activities and functional areas of businesses.

ii.   Functional level

Composed principally of:

- Managers of product areas

- Geographic areas

- Functional areas

Functions:-

1.   Develop annual objectives and short term strategies in such areas as;

·   Production

·   Operations

·   Research and development

·   Finance

·   Accounting

·   Marketing and

·   Human relations

2.   Implement and execute the firm's strategic plans.

Critical tasks comprising strategic management are to:-

·   Formulate the company's mission, including board statements about its purpose, philosophy and goals

·   Conduct an analysis that reflects the company's internal conditions and capabilities

·   Assess the company's external environment including both the competitive and the general contextual factors

·   Analyze the company's options by matching its resources with the external environment

·   Identify the most desirable options by evaluating each option in light of the company's mission

·   Select a set of long term objectives and grand strategies that will achieve the most desirable options

·   Develop annual objectives and short term strategies that are compatible with the selected set of long term objectives and grand strategies

·   Implement the strategic choices by means of budgeted resource allocations in which the matching of tasks, people, structures, technologies and reward system is emphasized

·   Evaluate the success of the strategic process as an input for future decision making.

iii.   Business level

    . composed principally of:-

    .business managers

    . corporate managers

Functions

1. translate the statement of which direction and intent generated at the corporate level into concentrated objectives and strategies for individual business divisions

2. determine how the form will complete in the selected product arena.

3. strive to identify and secure the most promising market segment within that arena.

Strategic controls:-

Every strategy is based on certain planning premises assumption or prediction:

i.   Premise control

Every strategy is based on certain planning premises- assumption or predictions. Premise control is designed to check systematically and continuously whether the premises on which the strategy is based are still valid. If a vital premise is no longer valid, the strategy may have to be changed.

Note: planning premises are primarily concerned with environmental and industrial factors; examples.

·   Environmental factors

Although a firm has little or no control over environmental factors, these factors exercise considerable influence over the success of its strategy, and strategies usually are based on key premises about them. Inflation, technology, interest rates, regulation, demographic and social changes are examples of such factors.

·   Industry Factors

The performance of the firms in a given industry is affected by industry factors. Competitors, suppliers, product substitutes and barriers to entry are a few of the industry factors about which strategic assumptions are made.

Managers must select premises whose change is likely and would have a major impact on the firm and its strategy.

· Strategic Surveillance

By their nature, premises controls are focused controls, strategic surveillance, however is unfocused. Strategic surveillance is designed to monitor a broad range of events inside and outside the firm that are likely to affect the course of its strategy. The basic idea behind strategic surveillance is that important yet unanticipated information may be unrecovered by a general monitoring of multiple information sources. Strategic surveillance must be kept as unfocused as possible.

· Special alert control

A special alert control is thorough, and often rapid, reconsideration of the firms strategy because of the sudden, unexpected event. The strategic events of World Trade Center (WTC) in US on September 11, 2001 caused many firms to reorganize their strategic plans.

· Implementation control

A special implementation takes place as a series of steps, programs, investments and moves that occur over an extended time. Special programs are undertaken. Functional areas initiate strategy related activities. Key people are added or reassigned. Resources are mobilized. In other words, managers implement strategy by converting broad plans into the concrete, incremental actions and results of specific units and individuals.

Advantages of strategic planning:-

i.   It provides a logical, systematic approach to dealing with the increasingly turbulent environment of the recent years

ii.   Complexity of modern organizations requires this type of planning

iii.   Since it involves several levels of management, it creates a valuable communication channel.

iv.   Strategizing enables management to forecast future happenings in the organization

v.   Organizations that enforce strategic planning exercises tend to maximize their production.

Limitations of strategic planning:-

i.   An intrinsic limitation is that strategic planning cannot ensure the selection of the most appropriate strategies, and hence the success of the organization.

ii.   The environment does not always turn out as forecast

iii.   Managers, even with appropriate data, do not always select the best alternatives

iv.   People tend to resist changes that alter their normal routine

v.   Planning is intellectually difficult. Most managers are by nature action oriented, they find it hard to exercise the patience and intellectual discipline required by serious planning

vi.   Most managers lack the necessary analytical skills

vii.   The cost associated with the planning can be enormous

viii.   The time associated with the planning can also be very high

Chapter 4/2: DECISION MAKING AND PROBLEM SOLVING

Introduction

In a business sense, a decision is usually the result of choosing between uncertainties. Often a decision is taken on the grounds of future projections and therefore is subject to uncertainty and risk. In this way, it can be seen that the decision making process is one involving value judgments and risk taking.

Definition

Decision making is selection from among alternative courses of action.

The law of principle of exception:-

This law states that each manager carries out the duties allocated to him and will make such decisions as is necessary which fall within his scope of authority. Only when decisions are required which lie outside his authority would he be expected to call in higher authority.

ii.   Reaction decision theory

Reaction decision theory assumes that once policies and corporate plans are established, decisions that are required follow as a natural result of those plans. In this way, decision making is regarded as an extension of the process of implementing corporate plans. Decisions therefore are partly predetermined by the details of the plans.

In real life situations, scientific and reaction decisions are usually made on the basis of facts but individual judgment will also be a major ingredient.

iii.   Marginal theory

This theory stresses on profit maximization. The economists who developed this theory say that profits will be maximum only when marginal costs of inputs are equal to marginal revenues. Marginal cost represents the additional cost of producing an additional unit and marginal revenue is the extra revenues for the product. When the marginal cost and revenue differ, the profit cannot be maximum. Either more additional revenues will be earned at less additional cost or vice versa. In practice, it is very difficult to locate the marginal point for each factor of production because these are carried on with the corporation of everyone in the organization.

iv.   Psychological theory

The thrust of this theory is on the maximization of customer satisfaction. The manager acts as an "administrative man" rather than "economic man". A good manager will try to protect economic interest of the enterprise besides maximizing consumer's satisfaction. According to this theory the consumer's interest should be a top priority in the mind of the decision maker.

v.   Mathematical theory

This theory is based in the use of models. This is also known as operations research theory. The techniques generally used include linear programming theory of probability, simulation models, games theory, network theory, etc. The analyst defines the problem area, uses symbols for unknown data and then tries to solve it. This theory is more systematic as compared to other theories.

Types of decisions

i.   Organizational and personal decisions.

Decisions taken by an executive in his official capacity or on behalf of the organization are known as the organizational decisions. The authority for taking such a decision can be delegated as such decisions have direct bearing on the functioning of the organization. Personal decisions are decisions taken by an individual for himself in his personal capacity and not on behalf of the firm. Decision-making power for personal decision cannot be delegated. Such decisions normally influence the personal life of the decision maker. In some cases it may affect the organization e.g. decision to leave the organization.

ii.   Routine and strategic decisions.

Routine or strategic decisions relate to the day-to- day operation. They are taken respectively in accordance with the established policies, practices and procedures. Routine decisions are normally taken at lower levels of management. Such decisions involve few alternatives and relates to the economic use of resources. The top management normally takes strategic decisions. They are concerned with policy matters and exercise fundamental influence on the objectives facilities and structure of the organization. Such decisions involve long-term commitments and therefore require careful analysis and considerate deliberations. Expensive considered opinions and operations research techniques are used in making such decisions.

iii.   Policy and operational decisions.

 Policy and operational decisions are of vital importance and they affect the entire organization. Top management undertakes them. Such decisions set forth the basic policies and general direction of the enterprise. Policy decisions are sometimes published in the form of a policy manual for the guidance of lower level of executives. Operating or administrative decisions are generally taken at lower level of management. They translate policies into specific actions that is the manner of executing the established policies. Policy decisions serve as basis of taking operating decisions.

iv.   Programmed and non-programmed decisions.

Programmed decisions are routine and repetitive by nature and they are dealt with according to specific procedures. Systematic procedures are established for such decisions so that the problem needs not to be treated as a unique case each time , for example application of leave. Non-programmed decisions are required to solve unstructured problems. They are non- repetitive and novel in nature. There exist no standard procedures for handling such problems and every decision is a unique case. Considerable judgment intuition and creativity are involved in such decisions.

v.   Individual and group decisions

Decisions may be taken by an individual or by a group of persons. A Decision taken by an individual or single person is known as individual decision. Individual decisions are taken in small organization or those organizations that operate under autocratic style of management. Individual decisions are taken in case of routine problems involving simple analysis of variables and in situations where definite procedures to deal with the problem already exist. Group decisions refer to a decision taken by a group e.g. board of directors, executive committee. A group generally takes important and strategic decisions. Group decision tends to be more balanced, acceptable and practicable but they involve greater expenditure of the money and effort. It is difficult to fix responsibility for such decisions.

Stages In Decision Making

Decision making is a systematic and planned process consisting of several interrelated phases. These various stages are:-

i.   Identifying and specifying the problem

The first step is to recognize, identify, determine and define the problem clearly A problem is half solved when it is well defined. Definition or perception of the problems involves the definition of desired results, identification of the fundamental cause and magnitude of the problem and the limits or boundaries within which it can be solved.

ii.   Analyzing the problem

Once the problem is defined, it must be analyzed in terms of nature, impact futurity periodically etc of the decision. Analysis of the problem also involves enumerations' of the limiting or static factors relevant to the decision. These are the major obstacles in achieving the results .They may be material, human or external factors. Such analysis is required to determine who should take the decision, what information is required and how it can be gathered.

iii.   Developing alternative solutions

 In order to make a decision, it is essential to search for and identify viable or possible alternative. Due to time and cost constraints, it is not possible to know all possible alternatives. This step requires considerable imagination, experience and judgment. The ability to develop a responsible number of alternatives is important as is making of a right choice among alternatives. Ingenuity, research and creativity are required to make sure that alternatives are considered before a course of action is selected. While listing alternative courses of action, the negative aspect should be ignored.

iv.   Evaluating alternatives

Alternatives are evaluated in terms of their cost, time feasibility and contribution to objectives. Alternative solutions should be assessed in terms of critical or limiting factors, both tangible and intangible. It is important to determine the action to be taken in solving a given problem. Managerial analysis and cost benefits analysis are helpful in the evaluation of alternatives. Evaluation involves deliberations or measurements or merits and demerits of various alternatives. The evaluation of the various alternative in terms of their strength and weakness in achieving the objectives must be as systematic and objectives as possible. The following internal observations can be used to evaluate the probable consequence of difficult alternatives:-

·   Risk: The manager should wash the risk involved in each course of action against the expected gains.

·   Economy of effort: an alternative is considered best, which leads to the realization of the goal with the minimum of time, money, efforts and with the least disturbance in the organization

·   Timing: if the situation has great urgency, the preferable course of action is one that warns the organization that something important is happening. But if consistence and long efforts are needed, a slow start that gathers momentum approach may be preferable.

·   Limitation of resources: the most important resources whose limitation has to be considered are the human beings who will carry out the decision. Effective implementation of the decision may require competence and skills, which are not available in the organization. Finance, materials and power may be other limiting resources.

v.   Selecting the last alternative

The alternative, which can make net maximum contribution to the goal, is selected. Selection is the point of ultimate decision making. While choosing the best alternative the following approaches may be used:-

·   Experience: In making a final decision a past experience in dealing with problems of a similar nature can be helpful if the experience is carefully analyzed rather than blindly followed and if fundamental reasons for success or failure are distilled from it.

·   Experimentation: Under this approach, the tentative decision is put into practice and the results observed. Various alternatives are tried and the alternative giving the best results is selected.

·   Research and analysis: This approach focuses its attention on different parts of the problem. However every problem may not lend itself to the use of this approach due to the cost and delays involved.

vi.   Implementing the decision

Implementation or execution of the decision involves development of detailed plans:-

·   Communication of the decision.

·   Gaining of acceptance.

·   Getting support and cooperation of those concerned for converting the decision into effective action and

·   Developing controls to ensure that the decision is being carried out properly.

vii.   Evaluation of the decision process

If the evaluation or follow up shows unsatisfactory results, the process should be reviewed and the decision may be modified. The review involves asking the following questions;

·   Was the problem really defined adequately in terms of objectives, constraints and measures of success?

·   Were pertinent alternatives and uncertainties identified?

·   Was relevant information obtained?

·   Was enough time spent on defining the problem and collecting information?

·   Was available information analyzed and interpreted logically?

·   Was the preferred alternative solution implemented properly?

The actual results of the decision and action should be compared with the expected results and the deviations, if any analyzed.

viii.   The feedback: The feedback obtained through the follow up of the decision will become the basis for necessary improvements in the decision making processes.

Problems In Decision Making

The efforts of management are to take correct decisions. A wrong decision at any level of management may create difficulties for the whole business. In spite of best efforts, there are certain problems in decision making. Some of these are discussed as follows:

i.   Correctness of decisions

Whether the decisions are taken or not, is the first problem faced by the management. If the decision is not correct then it will be a waste of money and efforts. The correctness of a decision depends on the caliber of decision maker, information available and its analysis. If proper facts and figures are not available then decision will be based on wrong premises.

When they are based on a correct problem and its proper analysis then decisions will not be correct.

ii.   Timing of decision

Timing of decisions is the other difficulty faced by management. It is important to take decisions at the most opportune time. The determination of that time in itself is a problem. The decisions will be in vain if not taken at right time.

iii.   Effective communication of decisions

The communication of decisions to the persons for whom they have been taken is another administrative problem faced by the management. The decisions should be communicated in language in which they are well understood by the receiver. If a decision is not conveyed to those who are to implement them, then it will remain on paper and the purpose will not be served. The management has to cross many barriers in the communication system so that they are conveyed properly.

iv.   Participation in decision making

The best way of arriving at important decisions is to get the views of concerned persons before finalizing them. Different viewpoints will give a wider thought to the problem and its analysis.

The general tendency in management is to keep decision making at a top level only. A few persons are given the authority of making decisions may not be taken into consideration. To avoid such situations management should try involving more and more persons in decision making process.

v.   Decision environment

The organizational and physical environment prevailing in the business will have an influence on decision making process. If the environment is conducive then there will be proper cooperation and mutual understanding among various persons. The decisions will be accepted in a good spirit and will be honestly implemented. It will also provide scope for research and creative thinking.

vi.   Implementation of decision

The implementation of decisions is the other difficulty faced by management. Once a decision is taken then all efforts should be made honestly to implement it. The manager and subordinates should help in proper implementation of decisions. Manager may consult staff persons or specialists from outside but final decision will be his own. The responsibilities for implementing decisions will lie on the manager. When a decision goes wrong then manager is criticized and when it proves correct then he may not be applauded. So decision implementation brings a number of problems which need to be tackled.

Group Decision Making

Groups such as committees, project teams or review panels often play a key role in the decision making process.

Advantages of group decision making

I. Greater pool of knowledge: A group can bring much more information and experience to bear on decision or problem than can an individual acting alone.

ii. Different perspectives: Individuals with varied experience and interests help the group see decision situations and problems from different angles.

iii. Greater comprehension: Those who personally experience the give and take of group discussion about alternative courses of action tend to understand the rational behind the final decision.

iv. Increased acceptance: Those who play an active role in group decision making and problem solving tend to view the outcome as "our" rather than theirs.

v. Training ground: Less experienced participants in group action learn how to cope with group dynamics by actually being involved.

Disadvantages of group decision making

i.   Expensive: participants use stationery and other times they are fed

ii.   Its time consumer especially when participants engage in disagreement.

iii.   Other times, participants develop conflict

iv.   Decisions, other times are likely to be of low quality

v.   Lack of accountability

Chapter 4/3: HUMAN RESOURCE PLANNING

Introduction

In recent years, more attention has been given to the importance of planning human resources as well as other economic resources such as capital, materials, machinery and equipment. At both the national and the organizational level, it is essential that human resources are utilized as effectively as possible. At the national level, the basic aim is to review performance in different industries in line with anticipated future economic growth. Government action is geared towards overcoming problems of overstaffing/understaffing and the movement (redeployment) of workers accordingly.

Definitions

I.   Human resource planning is defined as a strategy for the acquisition, utilization, improvement and retention of an organization's human resources.

ii.   Human resource planning is a process of forecasting an organization's future demand for and supply of the right types of people in the right number.

Main stages/ processes in HR planning:-

i.   An Analysis of existing staffing resources: This requires an effective system of personnel records and a staffing inventory.

ii.   An estimation of likely changes in resources by the target date: This includes consideration of changes and losses to the organization, increment improvements in staff performance and current programmes of staff development and external environmental factors such as the likely availability of labour: This determines the supply forecast.

iii. A forecast of staffing requirements necessary to achieve corporate objectives by the target date: This determines the demand forecast.

iv. A series of measures to ensure that the required staffing resources are available as and when required: This reconciliation of supply and demand is the basis of the human resource planning and the personnel management action programme.

v.   The human resource planning process should also take account of broader environmental factors, such as changes in population trends, patterns of employment for example, part time workers, level of competition from other organizations for example, labour force, changes in educational system, government initiatives on employment, training or enterprise programmes and employment legislation, developments in information technology and automation.

Principles/ requirements of an effective HR planning

i.   HR plan has to be fully integrated into the other areas of organization's strategy and planning

ii.   Senior management must give a lead in stressing its importance throughout the organization.

iii.   In larger organizations, a central human resource planning unit responsible to senior management may be established to enable the management co-ordinate and reconcile the demands for human resources from different departments

iv.   The time span to be covered by the plan needs to be defined

v.   The scope and details of the plan have to be determined

vi.   Human resource planning must be based on the most comprehensive and accurate information

Concepts of HR planning

The concepts of HR planning are basically straightforward and so are most of the methods involved. However, a number of more sophisticated statistical and quantitative techniques have been developed. Computer programmes are also available for more complex models of man power planning. These techniques can be helpful but should be applied only as appropriate to the amount of detail and accuracy required. What is most important is recognition of the need for effective HR planning to suit the requirements of the particular organization.

Advantages of human resource planning

i.   HR planning can assist organizations to foresee changes and identify trends in staffing resources.

ii.   HR planning adopts personnel policies which help to avoid major problems.

iii.   A human resource plan provides the trigger for a personnel management action programme aimed at reconciling differences between supply and demand.

iv.   HR planning provides a framework in which action can be taken to help overcome staffing difficulties facing the organization.

v.   HR planning is a continuous process which ensures flexible resourcing related to internal and external environmental influences.

vi.   Effective HR planning can help anticipate potential future difficulties while there is still a choice of action.

vii.   Forward planning enables the organization to develop effective personnel strategies related to such activities as; recruitment and selection, training and retraining, management development and career progression, transfer and redeployment, early retirement, wage/ salary levels, anticipated redundancies and accommodation requirements.

viii.   HR planning helps the organization create and develop employee training and management succession programmes.

ix.   HR planning estimates the size and makeup of the future work force in order to adjust supply of personnel to the demand.

Disadvantages of human resources planning

i.   Most of organizations are not able to develop effective succession planning programmes because of internal skills shortages.

ii.   Most organizations experience staff retention difficulties

iii.   Most organizations are negatively affected by women who decline to go back to work after maternity leave.

iv.   To remain effective, organizations are forced to spend more funds for training existing staff.

v.   Most organizations are not able to have effective human resource plans because of high rate of labour turnover caused by staff that resign to take up better paid jobs created by competitors.

vi.   The plan may indicate recruitment and training programmes which, although desirable, may be impossible to put into practice because the money to pay for them may not be available

vii.   The difficult of forecasting social and economic changes accurately, particularly in an era of high unemployment rate may adversely affect planners

viii. The rapid growth of new technologies adversely affects planners.

Chapter 4/4: ORGANIZATIONAL DEVELOPMENT (OD)

Introduction

The researchers in organizational development concept had the aim of improving every operation in the organization. They wanted customers to benefit from a better quality at a lower cost, workers to benefit from a more effective organizational climate and the organization to benefit from increased effectiveness.

Organizational development also seeks to change beliefs, attitudes, values, structures and practices so that the organization can better adapt to technology and live with the fast pace of change.

Definition

Organizational development is an intervention strategy that uses group processes to focus on the whole culture of an organization in order to bring about planned change.

Characteristics of OD

A number of techniques are implied in the definition of OD and these characteristics differ substantially from those in a typical training program. They are discussed in the following paragraphs.

I.   Focus on the whole organization

OD attempts to develop the whole organization so that it can respond to change effectively. Change is so abundant in modern society that organizations need all their parts working together in order to solve the problems and opportunities that are brought by change. OD is a comprehensive program that is intended to assure that all parts of the organization are well coordinated. More traditional training approaches tend to focus on specific jobs or small work groups.

ii.   Systems orientation

OD is concerned with interactions of various parts of the organization as they affect each other. It is concerned with working relationships as well as personal ones. It is concerned with structure and process as well as attitudes. The basic issue to which it is directed is, how do all these parts work together to be effective? Emphasis is on how the parts relate, not on the parts themselves.

iii.   Use of a change agent

OD uses one or more change agents, who are people with the role of stimulating and coordinating change within a group. Usually the primary change agent is a consultant from outside the company. In this way, the agent can operate independently without ties to the hierarchy and politics of the firm. The personnel director usually is the in house change agent who coordinates the program internally with both management and external agent. The external agent also works with management so that the result is a three way relationship of the personnel director, management and an outside consultant as they develop the OD program.

In rare cases the organization has its own in house professional consultant who replaces the outside one and works with the personnel director and management. This in house consultant usually is a specialist on the personnel staff.

iv.   Problem solving

OD emphasizes on problem solving. It seeks to solve problems rather than to discuss them theoretically as in a classroom. These problems are real ones that the participants face in their organization, so they are stimulating and interesting. This focus on real, ongoing problems, not artificial ones, is called action research. It is such a key characteristics that OD sometimes is defined as "organizational improvement through action research".

v.   Experiential learning

Experiential learning means that participants learn by experiencing in the training environment the kinds of human problems they face on the job. Then they can discuss and analyze their own immediate experience and learn from it. This approach tends to produce more changed behaviour than the traditional lecture and discussion in which people talk about abstract ideas. Theory is necessary and desirable, but the ultimate test is how it applies in a real situation. OD helps to provide some of the answers. Participants experiences help solidify, or referees new learning.

vi.   Group processes

OD relies on group processes such as group discussion, intergroup conflicts, confrontations and procedures for cooperation. There is an effort to improve interpersonal relations, open communication channels, build trust and encourage responsiveness to others.

vii.   Feedback

OD relies heavily on feedback to participants so that they will have concrete data on which to base decisions. Feedback encourages them to understand a situation and take self correcting action rather than wait for someone else to tell them what to do.

An example is a feedback exercise in one OD program;

Participants are separated into two groups representing two different departments in the organization. Both groups are asked to develop answers to the following questions:

·   What characteristics best describe our group?

·   How will the other group describe us?

After the separate groups have prepared their answers, they assemble and present their answers to the other group. They give concrete feedback about impression each group has of the other, and there are usually major misunderstandings. In this presentation no argument are allowed. Questions are accepted only to clarify what the other group is saying.

The groups again are separated to discuss two other questions

·   How did these misunderstandings occur?

·   What can we do to correct them?

With this new feedback, the groups meet to develop specific plans of action for solving their misunderstandings. In each instance feedback about themselves is the basis for their next activities.

viii.   Contingency orientation

OD usually is said to be situational and contingency oriented. Unlike many other training approaches that emphasize only one right way to deal with a problem, OD is flexible and pragmatic, adapting actions to fit particular needs, Although an occasional OD change agent may try to impose a single best way on the group, usually there is open discussion of several better alternatives rather than a single best way.

ix.   Team building

The general goal of OD is to build better teamwork throughout the organization. Both small and large group teams are emphasized. Obviously small task teams must work together to be effective, but also cooperation is needed among all of the small teams that make up the whole institution. OD attempts to tie all these groups into one integrated, cooperative group. For example, if the production and marketing departments are not working together, OD attempts to integrate into an effective unit the four elements of people, structure, technology and environment. The result should improve organizational performance.

Benefits of organizational development

i.   It encourages change throughout the organization.

ii.   It motivates the workers in the whole organization.

iii.   It encourages workers to maximize production.

iv.   Workers are encouraged to improve quality of work.

v.   It increases workers job satisfaction.

vi.   It enhances employees' team spirit.

vii.   It encourages commitment to objectives.

viii.   It causes the reduction of the rate of labour turn over.

ix.   It causes the reduction of the rate of tardiness (tardiness-absenteeism from the working desk while an employee is still in the organization)

Disadvantages of organizational development

i.   Introduction of organization development programme is very expensive.

ii.   To introduce organization development programme is time consumer.

iii.   There is no assurance that organization development programme would succeed.

iv.   There is likelihood of leakage of organization information especially when a change agent is included.

ORGANIZATIONAL DEVELOPMENT TECHNIQUES

Organizational development techniques provide the means that adequately transfer the learned techniques to the job situation and also provide participants with the desire and qualifications that motivate them to follow expected patterns of behaviour.

Types of organization development techniques:-

i.   Sensitivity training (T-group Training)

An OD technique that uses leadership groups. The general goal of sensitivity training is to develop awareness of and sensitivity to oneself and others. More specifically, the goals of sensitivity training include:

- Increased openness with others

- Greater concern for needs of others

- Increased tolerance for individual differences

- Less ethnic prejudice

- Awareness and understanding of group processes

- Enhanced listening skills

- Greater appreciation of the realistic personal standard of behaviour.

Research investigations into sensitivity training indicate that it can effectively change individual behaviour. Its impact on performance is inconclusive and the technique is not devoid of psychological risks. Sensitivity training is not widely used in business today as an OD technique. Leaders of T-groups have been criticized as having an insufficient background in psychology. Detractors have suggested that in business organizations, managers frequently must make unpleasant decisions that work to the detriment of particular individuals and groups. Excessive empathy and sympathy will not necessarily lead to a better decision and may exact an excessively high emotional cost for the decision maker. Many business organizations have commanding and autocratic leadership. The power structure may not be compatible with openness and trust. In some instances, effective managers may practice diplomacy by telling only part of the truth or perhaps even telling different stories to two different persons or groups. Truth is not always conducive to effective interpersonal and group relations. Sensitivity training would also tend to ignore organizational values that are derived from aggressiveness, initiative and charismatic appeals of a particular leader.

Theories of decision making

i.   Scientific decision theory

Scientific decision making depends on the quantitative techniques to management. In this way, attempts are made to measure and express all viable alternatives. This approach depends upon the view that complete information will lead to the 'ideal solutions'.

ii.   Organizational task laboratory (OTL)

This is a laboratory like sensitivity training. The basic component of the techniques is a small group composed of between 5 and 15 people. In the OTL, representative management situations and decisions are created with the hope of allowing managers and the work group to experience and learn about:-

·   Recognition of conflict: the emphasis here is placed on how management can work more effectively with their groups and with other managers so as to increase individual and goal accomplishment.

·   Reconsideration of established practices: the participants are encouraged to examine their own behavioral styles and those of others.

·   Formulation of explicit goals: the OTL stresses importance of explicit, clear objectives and their advantages over vague guidelines.

·   Experimentation groups are designed to encourage participants to experiment and innovate and means of evaluating the consequences of creative action.

Compared to sensitivity training, organization task laboratory places more emphasis on task oriented team experience and less on self awareness and sensitivity in interpersonal relations. OTL emphasizes on group problem solving. Members of various units come together to utilize group processes in formulating goals and experimenting with innovative ways of accomplishing them. Groups are often capable of stimulating individual behaviour in positive or functional directions.

iii.   Survey feedback

The method of basing organizational change efforts on the systematic collection and measurement of subordinate attitudes by anonymous questionnaires. The three basic steps in the process are, data collection, feedback to organizational units and action decisions. Surveys are typically either the objective multiple choice type or disagreement with a particular question. Normally, anonymously answered questionnaires are used. If truthful information concerning attitudes is to be obtained, the employee must feel comfortable, secure and confident in responding.

In the second step, the results of the study are presented to concerned organizational units. In the final step, the data are analyzed and decisions are made. Means by which the data may be compared and analyzed include: scores by organizational level, scores by seniority, relative scores on each question and scores for each question.

The decisions are directed at improving relationships in the organization. This is accomplished by revealing problem areas and dealing with them through straight forward discussions.

iv.   Transactional analysis (T.A)

An OD technique used as a means of improving relationships between individuals. Attempt is made to analyze the social interchanging (transaction) among people with the objectives of understanding and eventually improving interpersonal relations. When a person through transactional analysis learns to perceive his state or that of others, relations can be better understood and the transaction improved.

As an OD technique, transaction analysis encourages organizational members to act more as adults and less as children or parents, thus making them more receptive to change and capable of responding in a mature manner.

v.   Confrontation meetings

Organizational confrontation meetings is an OD technique designed to mobilize the resources of the organization towards problem identification, the establishment of priorities and goals, and an action plan for accomplishing them. This technique is frequently used when an organization experiences significant personnel changes. The process is well defined.

. A group is informed of the situation and assigned the task of identifying the problems facing the organization. Individuals are then assigned to heterogeneous groups and asked in an honest and open way to identify organizational problems. The groups then come back together as a larger group and each segment reports each list of problems and may propose solutions.

. The leader (change agent) then classifies the problem and the larger group is broken down into homogenous segments e.g. marketing personnel are assigned marketing problems, financial managers assigned financial problems, etc . The groups then establish priorities and suggest solutions of plans of action.

. The groups periodically report their progress and receive feedback from other units. Periodic meetings are scheduled to keep all areas of the organization informed about the progress being made. Confrontation meeting techniques appears particularly valuable in bringing total resources of an organization to beat on the solution of common problems. It provides employees with a feeling of participation in the problem solving operation.

vi.   Management by objectives (MbO)

MbO is an OD technique which is systematic approach that facilitates achievement of results and of directing effort towards attainable goals. MbO is a philosophy of management that encourages managers to plan for the future. Because MbO emphasizes participative management approaches, it has been called a philosophy of management. Within this broader context, MbO becomes an important method of OD. The participation of individuals in setting goals and the emphasis on self control, promotes not only individual's development but also development for the entire organization.

vii. Team building

One of the major techniques in the arsenal of organization development consultancy is team building. Team building is a conscious effort to development of effective work groups throughout the organization. The focus of the team building is the development of effective management teams. These work groups focus on solving actual problems in building efficient management teams. The team building process begins when the team leader defines a problem that requires organizational change. Next, the group analyzes the problem to determine the underlying causes. These factors may be related to such areas as communication, role clarifications, leadership styles, organizational structure and interpersonal frictions. The next step is to propose alternative solutions and then select the most appropriate one. Through this process the participants are likely to be committed to the solution. Interpersonal support and trust develops. The overall improvement is the interpersonal support and trust of group members and enhances the implementation of the change. The concept of the quality circle, imported from Japan, is a modern example of team building.

viii.   Job enrichment

The deliberate restructuring of a job to make it more challenging, meaningful and interesting is referred to as job enrichment. The individual is provided with an opportunity to derive greater achievement, recognition, responsibility and personal growth in performing the job.

Job enrichment is vertical expansion of jobs so that employees take on additional responsibilities to plan, execute and inspect their work. Successful job enrichment also increases freedom and independence of employees, organize tasks so as to allow workers to do a complete activity and provide feedback so that individuals can be able to correct their own performance. A successful job enrichment program should ideally increase employee satisfaction but organizations do not exist to create employee satisfaction as an end, there must be also direct benefits to the organization.

ix.   Managerial Grid

One of the best known redesigned OD programs is the management grid by Robert Blake and Jane Mouton. Blake and Mouton suggest that the most effective leadership style is that which stresses maximum concern for both output and people. The managerial grid provides a systematic approach for analyzing managerial styles and assisting the organization in moving to the best style.

The parameters of organizational development are not clearly defined. Instead, OD is impartial in the sense that it chooses from a variety of tools, methods and techniques that are suitable to facilitate the solving of particular enterprise problems

Conditions for successful OD program:-

i.   Recognition by managers and members that the organization has problems: Without such recognition, it is unlikely a change process will receive the required resources to make the effort successful.

ii.   Use of an external change agent to start the process: The change agent should not be a member of the organization. Internal change agents often lack the objectivity and autonomy to carry out necessary changes, and their efforts may be hampered by political infighting.

iii.   Support from top management for the change process: Top management must support the program.

iv.   Involvement of work group leaders: The work group leaders must have an active role in the change process.

v.   Human resource managers should be included in the OD program.

vi.   The change agent should watch and respond to situations to optimize the chances of success.

vii.   Staff should be made to understand the change process and its goals.

viii.   The change agent should involve and train organization managers at all levels in OD skills and techniques.

        Benefits of OD:-

i.   Enhances change throughout organization.

ii.   Increases staff motivation.

iii.   Increases productivity.

iv.   Improves quality of work.

v.   Increases staff job satisfaction.

vi.   Strengthens   staff team work.

vii.   Enables management to solve conflicts easily

viii.   Encourages management and staff to be committed to objectives.

ix.   Increases staff willingness to change.

x.   Reduces staff rate of absenteeism.

xi.   Lowers percentage of the rate of labour turn over.

Limitation of OD:-

i.   Major time requirements.

ii.   Substantial expenses.

iii.   Delayed payoff period.

iv.   Possible failure.

v.   Possible invasion of privacy.

vi.   Possible physiological harm.

vii.   Emphasis on group process rather than performance.

viii.   Possible conceptual ambiguity

Chapter 4/5: ORGANIZATIONAL STRUCTURES

An organization structure is the sum total of the ways in which it divides its labour into distinct tasks and then achieves coordination between them (Mintzberg, 1979).

Steps in the organizational structure

The following are the steps to be followed:

i.   Determination of objectives: The objectives to be achieved are identified.

ii.   Determination, identification and enumeration of activities.

iii.   Grouping and assigning of activities: All similar activities are grouped together and assigned on the basis of divisions or departments. These groupings might be done on the basis of such primary functions such as production, marketing, and so on, or may be done on a derivative basis such as types of customers, geographical area and so on.

iv.   Delegation of authority: People assigned particular activities and responsibilities are assigned the necessary authority for performing these duties. Responsibility and authority are tied together.

Types of organization structure

1. Functional organization structure

Functional organization structure is a structure that groups' people together on the basis of their technical and specialist expertise (see the diagram below)

diagram

Advantages of functional organization structure:-

i.   It groups people together on the basis of their technical and specialized expertise.

ii.   The organization facilitates utilization and coordination of services in the whole enterprise.

iii.   It achieves efficiency through specialization.

iv.   Differentiates and delegates day to day operating decisions.

v.   Tightly links structure to strategy by designating key activities as separate units

vi.   Functional grouping provides better opportunities for career development.

vii.   Employees who are functionally grouped become experts in their operations which reduce their fatigue.

viii.   Workers in a functional organization structure tend to be more cohesive.

Disadvantages of a functional organizational structure

i.   It encourages development of sectional interests which may conflict with the needs of the organization as a whole

ii.   Functional structures are only best suited in a stable environment

iii.   Functional structures find it hard to diversify their products

iv.   Promotes narrow specialization and functional rivalry or conflict

v.   Creates difficulties in functional coordination and inter functional decision making

vi.   Limits development of general managers

2. Product based structured

This is a type of structure which groups its operations according to products. It is a popular structural form in a large organization having a wide range of products or services. (See diagram below)

diagram

Advantages of a product based structure

I.   It enables the diversification to take place.

ii.   It copes better with problems of technological change.

iii.   By grouping staff with similar expertise and their specialized equipment in one major unit, management effectively controls equipment and staff.

iv.   Continuous utilization of equipment by staff enables them to be experts.

v.   By grouping staff in the product based structure, it enables staff to reduce fatigue.

Disadvantages of product based structure

I. Each general manager may promote his own group products to the detriment of other parts of the company

ii. Top management is forced to spend valuable time controlling general managers

iii. Close control by top management tends to demotivate general managers.

iv. By continuing working in the product- based areas, managers are deprived of the chance to know the operations in other departments.

v. Managers tend to develop empire building mentality due to excessive experience acquired in product based department.

vi. Specialization in product based department blunts manager's initiative.

3. Geographically based structure

This structure groups its operations on a geographical basis. It is usually adopted where the realities of a national or international network of activities make some kind of regional structure essential for decision making and control. (See diagram below)

diagram

Advantages of geographically based structure

I. It easily adapts the realities of national or international network of activities

ii. Network of activities make some kind of regional structure essential for decision making

iii.   Regionally structured networks facilitate in control of activities effectiveness.

iv.   Improves functional coordination within the target market

v.   Provides excellent training grounds for higher level general managers

vi.   Takes advantage of economies of local operations

vii.   Allows tailoring of strategy to the needs of each geographic market

viii.   Delegates profit/ loss responsibility to lowest strategic level.

Disadvantages of geographically based structure

I.   Makes it more difficult to maintain consistent company positive image/ reputation

ii.   Management spends a lot of funds by engaging services of senior functional managers at headquarters to provide direction and guidance to line managers in the regions.

iii. Poses problem of deciding whether headquarters should impose geographic uniformity or geographic diversity should be allowed.

iv. Can result in duplication of staff services at headquarters and district level.

4. Divisionalised structure

This is a structure which is divided into divisions on the basis of products and/or geography.

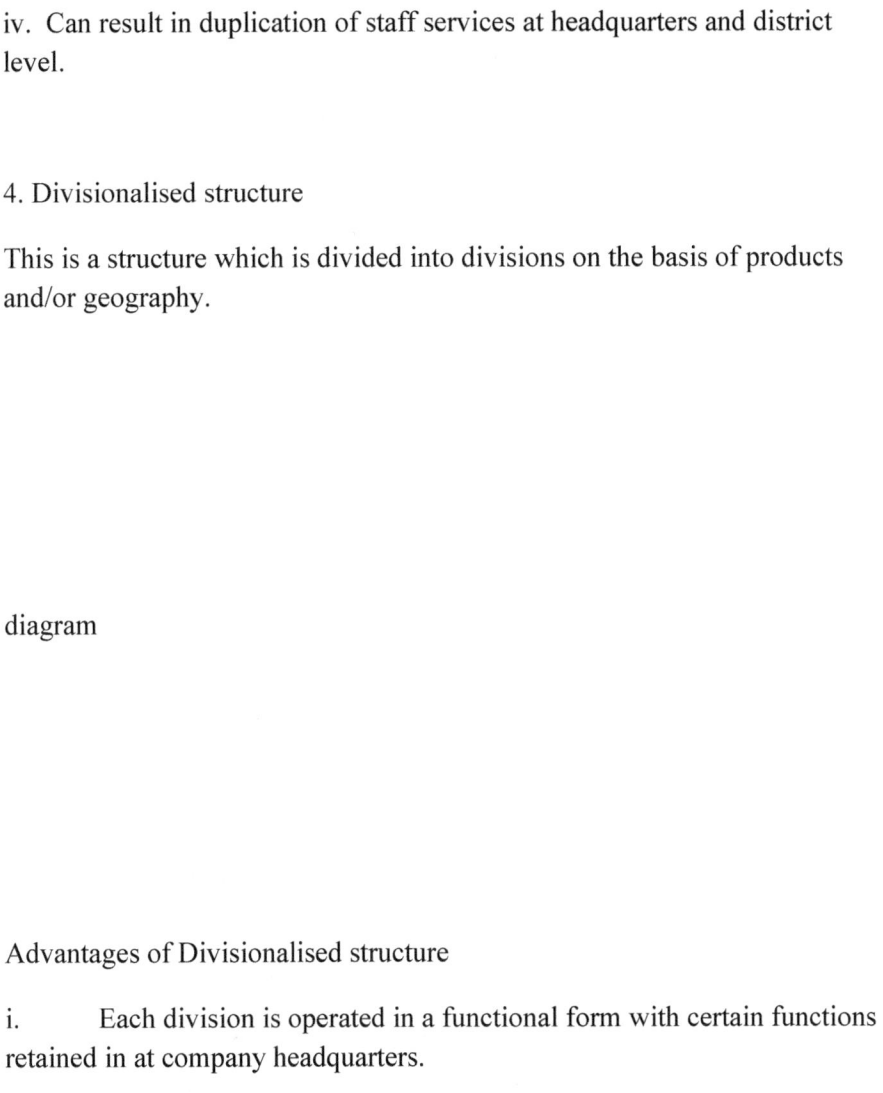

diagram

Advantages of Divisionalised structure

i.   Each division is operated in a functional form with certain functions retained in at company headquarters.

ii.   The structure is suitable for highly diversified firms operating in more than one country.

iii.   Regions in divisionalised structure control themselves and also market products developed by the parent company

iv.   Research and development activities and key corporate standards are controlled worldwide by a team of functional managers.

v.   Headquarters division provides group policy in key areas such as finance and personnel.

vi.   Frees chief executive officer for broader strategic decision making

vii.   Provides good training grounds for strategic managers

viii.   Increases focus on products, market and quick response to change

Disadvantages of divisionalised structure

i.   Divisionalised structure is not ideal for a small organization

ii.   Because regions in divisionalised structures control themselves, the chief manager in the headquarters will not know what is happening in the regions

iii.   Staff members in the divisionalised structures are not cohesive because of its very large size.

iv.   Group policy formulated in headquarters affecting finance and personnel departments is not able to serve regions effectively.

v.   Increases costs incurred through duplication of functions.

vi.   Enhances potential of policy inconstencies among divisions.

5.   Matrix structure

These structures have been developed to coordinate activities in highly complex industries such as aircraft manufactures where functional and product types of structures have not been able to meet organizational demands.

Matrix structure usually combines a functional form of structure with a project based structure.

(See diagram below)

diagram

Advantages of matrix structures:-

i.   Matrix structures combines lateral with vertical lines of communication and authority

ii.   Combination of lateral with vertical lines of communication and authority stabilizes the operations.

iii.   Matrix structures help to clarify who is responsible for the success of the project.

iv. Matrix structures focus on the requirements of the projects groups, which have direct contact with the clients.

v.   Matrix structure encourages functional managers to understand their contributive efforts.

vi. Manager's development of individual 'empire building mentality' is discouraged because each manager understands his contributive role.

vii. Provides excellent training for project managers running a diversified organization.

viii. Ensures that functional expertise is equally available to all projects.

ix. Makes maximum use of a limited pool of functional specialists.

Disadvantages of matrix structures:-

i.   Potential conflicts arise concerning the allocation of resources between project groups and functional specialists.

ii.   Matrix structures dilute functional managers' responsibilities throughout the organization.

iii.   Matrix structures encourage division of loyalties on the part of members of project teams in relation to their own managers and their functional superiors.

iv.   Slows down decision making process.

v.   Authority and responsibilities of managers may overlap which would lead to development of conflict among managers.

Benefits of a good organization structure:-

i.   A good structure facilitates attainment of objectives through proper coordination of all activities.

ii.   Conflicts between individuals over jurisdiction are kept to a minimum

iii.   It eliminates overlapping and duplication of work.

iv.   It facilitates promotions of personnel by pinpointing the positions of individuals relative to one another.

v.   It aids wage and salary administration by allowing a fair and equitable wage and salary base.

vi.   Communication is easier at all levels of organizational hierarchy since the line of communication and flow of authority is clearly identified on the organization chart.

vii.   It provides a sound basis for effective planning since the goals are clearly established and resources clearly identified.

viii.   A good structure eliminates ambiguity.

Chapter 4/6: JOB DESIGN/REDESIGN

Definition

It is an outgrowth of job analysis that improves jobs through technological and human considerations in order to enhance organization efficiency and employee job satisfaction.

Basis of job designs

Job design is a combination of four basic considerations:

i.   The organization objectives the job was created to fulfill. This includes task, duties and responsibilities to be performed.

ii.   Industrial engineering considerations including ways of making the job technologically efficient.

iii.   Ergonomic concerns, including workers physical and mental capabilities.

iv.   Behavioral concerns that influence employee's job satisfaction.

Job description as the central feature of the contract

i.   For the individual employees, the design of his job specifies the content and nature of his contribution to work activities and many of the conditions within which the work is carried out.

ii.   For the organization, job design determines the allocation of work, including supervision and integration between the different job holders in the organization.

iii. For both parties to the contract, job design is important for the utilization of individual abilities and skills, satisfaction with mutual expectations about work and the achievement of goals and objectives through work.

Job design methods:-

1. Job specialization

Job specialization is the process of the engagement of management and workers in concentration upon specific functional activities involving a limited range of task for which the individual's abilities and training enable expert performance.

2. Functional specialization

In this method individual job content is determined by a rational sub-division of organization work activities and is associated with precisely defined limits of responsibility and discretion. Managerial work involves specialization by administrative functions of planning, control, coordination and expert knowledge.

3.   Simplification

In this method, individual job content is limited as much as possible by minimizing the number of tasks and restricting variations in method and timing of operations.

This method is common in semi skilled jobs, particularly production line work, using work study and man machine systems design.

4. Job rotation

Job rotation is a process of moving an individual from one job another so as to enable him to perform variety of activities. The rotation may be voluntary, implying some degree of personal choice, but it usually obligatory with specification of time intervals and the task involved.

Advantages of job rotation

i.   Basic work processes remain undisturbed.

ii.   Covers for lateness and absenteeism.

iii.   With supervisory or management staff, it may make work more interesting.

iv.   It may be a basis for training in preparation for promotion.

v.   Rotation potentially provides the individual with opportunities for increased responsibility.

vi.   Job rotation reduces the degree of boredom.

vii.   It enables the rotated person to acquire varied skills.

viii.   It enables the rotated person to acquire varied experience.

5. Job enlargement

Job enlargement represents a definite movement away from simplified jobs, by extending the job content to include a wider range of tasks.

Advantages of job enlargement

i.   It reduces boredom of work.

ii.   It increases workers' job satisfaction.

iii.   With a larger number of tasks per worker, the time cycle of work increases, so reducing repetition.

iv.   Interest is considered to be developed by broader skill utilization.

v.   Broadened work skills of employees improve flexibility.

vi.   It is easier to introduce product changes or new models by changing the number of employees working on specific products.

6. Job enrichment

Job enrichment is a process of enhancing a job by adding more meaningful tasks and duties to make the work more rewarding or satisfying.

Factors for enriching jobs and thereby motivating employees include:-

i.   Achievement

ii.   Recognition

iii.   Growth

iv.   Responsibility

v.   Performance of the whole job versus only part of the job (Fredrick Herzberg)

Approaches used by managers to enrich employees' jobs:-

i.   Increasing the level of difficulty and responsibility of the job

ii.   Providing unit or individually job performance reports directly to employees

iii.   Allowing employees to retain more authority and control over work outcomes.

iv.   Adding new tasks to the job that require training and growth

v.   Assigning individuals specific tasks, thus enabling them to become experts.

7. Employee empowerment

Definition

Employee empowerment is a process of granting employees power to initiate change, thereby encouraging them to take charge of what they do.

Techniques of employee empowerment

I. Suggestion schemes

Employees are encouraged to take part in suggestion schemes. They are advised to forward their suggestions to the management. Employees get motivated when their suggestions are accepted and implemented.

ii. Innovation

The environment must be receptive to people with innovative ideas and encourage them to explore new paths and to take reasonable risks at reasonable tasks.

iii. Joint consultative committee

Employees representative solve the problems together with management representatives. This technique builds employees confidence.

8. Employees and managers attend a seminar together. This technique build employees confidence and also enable them to improve their performance skills.

Chapter 4/7: CONCEPTS OF EFFECTIVE AND EFFICIENT ORGANIZATION

Introduction

The main goal of every organization is to achieve the intended goal in a harmonious environment.

Organizations need to be efficient and effective in doing the right things, in the optimum use of their resources. Performance should be related to such factors as increasing profitability and improved service delivery.

Factors influencing organizational effectiveness and efficiency:-

1. Ability of the manager, for example,

i.   Strong personality

A manager must have strong personality. Managers with weak personality are not able to mobilize workers towards achieving the goal.

ii.   Positive attitude

Most managers fail because of having negative attitude. Negative attitude lowers the effectiveness of the manager leading to the failure of achieving the intended goal.

iii.   Relevant training

For a manager to succeed, one should have relevant training. Most managers fail to achieve their goals because of being placed on desks in which functions are completely irrelevant to their training.

iv.   Relevant experience

Some managers are given jobs in which they have little or no experience at all. Managers therefore, should be placed on desks in which have relevant experience so as to achieve effectiveness and efficiency.

v.   Ideal age

After training which is conducted after education, the trained manager increases his age. Very young managers find it hard to manage elderly workers. Managers, therefore, are supposed to have ideal age, perhaps over twenty five year to be able to effectively manage hence achieve the intended goal.

2. Economic environment

i.   Fair competition

For a manager to achieve effectiveness in his work, he is expected to work in an environment in which competition is fairly enforced. A manager cannot achieve effectiveness in an environment in which competition is unfairly enforced. For instance, reducing price so as to have an advantage over his competitor who is not able to reduce his price.

ii.   Strong economy

A manager working in an environment that enjoys strong economy is able to achieve his goal at the expected time frame.

iii.   Availability of resources

It is not possible for a manager to achieve effectiveness if one does not have necessary resources at his disposal.

3. Physical environment

i.   Ideal location

For a manager to succeed, he is supposed to work in an organization which is located in an ideal place. For example, Nairobi city is an ideal location because managers are easily able to get in touch with North, East, West and South (NEWS) events .Therefore, managers in Nairobi and other well placed locations easily achieve their goals.

ii.   Availability of amenities

Amenities such as recreation facilities, playgrounds are necessary. After work, managers need to take part in games and other leisure activities to reduce their stress which enable them to achieve effectiveness and efficiency.

iii.   Safety

Managers and employees that operate in safe environment are able to concentrate in their work which enable them to achieve effectiveness and efficiency.

iv.   Ideal climate

Managers and employees that operate in climates that are not favourable are not able to achieve effectiveness and efficiency.

v.   Ideal layout

For a business to succeed, the manager and employees are supposed to work in a business which is in an ideal location.

4. Group relations

i.   The span of control should be reasonable. Large groups find it hard to achieve their goals.

ii.   Group members are expected to be of reasonable age. Very young people are likely not able to be cohesive and therefore are not able to be effective and efficient.

iii.   Managers are supposed to set achievable goals. Very ambitious goals overwork employees which cause them not to achieve effectiveness and efficiency.

iv.   Some leaders are not effective and therefore cannot achieve effectiveness. Management is therefore supposed to engage the services of effective managers.

v.   The manager should allocate understandable tasks. Very difficult tasks stress workers which lead to the failure of achieving effectiveness and efficiency.

5.   Leadership

I.   To achieve effectiveness, the manager must have relevant knowledge and skills.

ii.   The manager/ leader should be able to enforce the right leadership style in different situations.

iii.   The manager should allocate achievable tasks.

iv.   He manager/ leader should establish a strong power base.

v.   To achieve effectiveness, the manager should allocate understandable tasks.

6. Systems and structures

So as to achieve effectiveness, the manager/ leader should establish:

i.   Efficient administrative structure

ii.   Fair control system

iii.   Ideal reward system

iv.   A strong power base - this can be achieved by treating all members of staff impartially

v.   Encourage staff to co-operate among themselves so as to develop a strong team

7. Motivation to work

i.   Workers should be promoted fairly and only due to their qualification and experience.

ii.   Employees that perform excellently well should be rewarded.

iii.   All staff should be trained if the management expects to achieve effectiveness.

iv.   Good offices with all required facilities should be allocated to employees.

v.   Employees should be paid better salaries to motivate them to work harder.

Technology environment

i.   Current and efficient technology should be introduced in the organization to enable the manager to improve their efficiency.

ii.   There should be qualified technicians to repair the equipment promptly when the need arises..

iii.   The equipment should be durable.

iv.   Equipment should have high resale value

v.   Equipment should have low depreciation rate.

vi.   There should be effective operators.

vii.   The equipment should be multi – purpose so as to accomplish various functions simultaneously

viii.   There should be plenty of spare parts to facilitate repairing faulty equipment promptly.

CHAPTER FIVE

GROUPS AND TEAMS IN ORGANIZATIONS

Definition of a group

i.   A group is any collection of people who perceive themselves as a group.

ii.   A group is also defined as a collection of individuals who have a similar objective.

Group development stages (Tuckman, 1965)

1.   Forming

Contents

i.   Establishment of tasks

ii.   Establishment of rules and regulations

iii.   Acquisition of resources

iv.   Identification of a leader

v.   Formulation of group policy

2.   Storming

Contents

Internal conflict develops when:

i.   Some or all members refuse to perform tasks

ii.   Some or all members fail to obey rules and regulations

iii.   Some or all members misuse resources

iv.   Some or all members refuse to obey the leader

v.   Some or all members refuse to accept the formulated policy

3.   Norming

Contents

i.   Conflict is settled

ii.   Co-operation develops

iii.   Views are exchanged freely

iv.   New standards or (norms) are developed.

4.   Performing

Contents

i.   Team work is achieved

ii.   Roles are played in a flexible manner

iii.   Solutions to problems are found

iv.   Solutions to problems are implemented.

Characteristics of Effective groups

i.   Members tend to be informal and portray a relaxed atmosphere

ii.   Members are committed to the achievement of targets and organizational goals.

iii.   Members have clear understanding of group's work

iv.   Members have clear understanding of the role of each person within the group

v.   Group members freely communicate among themselves.

vi.   Group members express their ideas freely and openly

vii.   Group members help each other by offering constructive criticisms and suggestions

viii. Conflict among group members is not avoided but brought into the open and dealt with constructively.

ix.   Group members seek consensus of opinion

x.   The group is sufficiently motivated to be able to carry on working in the absence of its leader.

Reasons for joining groups;

I. Task accomplishment

ii. Security: people will feel secure when they are in a group

iii. Self esteem: when a person is accepted by a group, his self esteem need is enhanced

iv. Group membership enhances member's status

v.   A member will feel proud when one is accepted by the group

vi. When one is accepted by a group, one feels important

vii. A person will join a group to reduce the degree of loneliness

viii. Group membership builds member's image

Formal groups

Definition

Formal groups in an organization are those which have been consciously created to accomplish the organization's collective purpose.

Functions of formal groups are:-

I. Test and ratify decisions made outside the organization

ii. Consult, negotiate and resolve disputes within the organization

iii. Create and exchange ideas.

iv. Coordinate the work of different individuals

v. Help individuals to develop images of themselves

vi. Motivate individuals to devote more energy and effort in to achieving the organization's goals.

vii. Spread the policy of the organization

viii. They enable individuals to help each other in matters which are not necessarily connected with the organization's purpose

ix. Satisfy social needs for friendship and belonging

Characteristic of formal groups:-

I. They have a formal structure.

ii. They are task oriented.

iii. They tend to be permanent until they accomplish their assignments.

iv. Their activities contributed directly to the organization's collective purpose.

v. They are consciously organized by somebody for a reason.

vi. They have defined rules and regulations.

vii. They are managed by officially appointed heads.

viii. They put emphasis on authority, functions, status differentials and down ward communication.

ix. They are based on delegation of authority and may grow to giant size.

Informal groups

Definition

I. An informal group is a collection of individuals who become a group when members develop interdependencies, influence one another's behavior and contribute to their mutual need satisfaction

ii. It is an unofficial structure which arises naturally without having been sanctioned by management.

Factors that influence development of informal groups:-

I. Tribal factor: People of the same tribe tend to have very close relations which isolate them from other people. They also tend to favour people of their tribe.

ii. Marital status: Married people tend to be closer to each other hence isolate unmarried ones.

iii. Profession: People of the same profession tend to be closer to each other than those in other professions.

iv. Age group: People tend to be more cohesive when they are in the same age group. They tend to relate well with those who are in their age group.

v. Gender: People of the same gender tend to be closer to each other than others

vi. Interest: People become very united when they have similar interest. They isolate others who have different interest.

vii. Culture: People that have the same culture tend to be more cohesive than those who have different culture

viii. Clan: People will become cohesive when they belong to the same clan.

ix. Race: People of different races tend to group themselves according to their races hence isolate those who do not belong to their races.

Characteristics of an informal group:-

I. It has no definite shape or structure.

ii. It has no clear division of work.

iii. It arises through social interactions between the members.

iv. It has unwritten rules and regulations.

v. It has no authorized organizational chart.

vi. It arises to satisfy members social satisfaction.

vii. It has no clear defined goals.

viii. It is formed by people who have similar objectives which are not organizational centered.

ix. One person can be a member of different informal groups in the same organization.

Types of informal groups

I. Teams: Football teams, volleyball teams are some of the informal groups found in the organizations.

ii. Unions: Trade unions e.g. COTU, Christian unions, political unions e.g. KANU are some of the informal groups found in the organizations.

iii. Clubs: Managers clubs, football clubs are some of the informal groups found in the organizations.

iv. Associations: Manufacturers normally register their associations to cater for their problems.

v. Societies: Societies like savings and credit societies are established to cater for workers employed in the same organization.

Advantages of informal groups

I. Informal group members can reveal negative activities of the management. The revelation of the negative activities force management to drop them.

ii. Management identifies well informed and reasonable employees during the bickering period.

iii. Employees in informal groups are very cohesive and therefore their production is high and of better quality.

iv. Management will economize on recruitment expenditure because many people will directly apply for jobs in the organization due to the organization's positive image caused by dropping of negative activities by the management.

v. Relations between management and employees improve after their differences are resolved.

vi. The rate of the labour turnover declines when the management perform its functions positively.

Disadvantages of informal groups

I. During the period members are bickering, the production is adversely affected.

ii. Management and informal group members develop poor relations which contribute to reduction of outputs.

iii.   Sometimes informal group members destroy property of the organization especially during strikes.

iv.   When management and informal group members differ, some members leak trade secrets to competitors.

v.   Continuous differences between management and informal group members, adversely affect the image of the organization.

vi.   Poor relations between management and informal group members cause the inflation of the rate of labour turnover.

Group cohesion

Definitions

i.   Group cohesion is defined as the sum of all the factors influencing members to stay in the group.

ii.   Group cohesion is also defined as that property which is inferred from the number and strength of mutual positive attitudes among members of the group (A.J Lott and B.E Lott, 1965)

Symptoms of cohesive groups

Cohesive groups display the following characteristic;

i.   Members have high degree of trust.

ii.   Members have high degree of job satisfaction.

iii.   Members freely communicate among themselves.

iv.   Group members have high rate of production.

v.   Members resist change.

vi.   Members respect each other.

vii. Members understand each other.

viii. Members like each other.

ix. Members observe punctuality.

x. Members support each other.

Factors that influence the development of group cohesiveness:-

i.   Similarity of attitude: people who have similar attitude tend to be cohesive.

ii.   Similar goals: people whose goals are similar tend to be cohesive.

iii.   Work assignment: people who have been given an assignment that is tailor-made tend to consult each other.

iv.   External threats: external threats unite people so as to overcome the foreseen threat.

v.   Reward systems: people become cohesive so as to benefit from rewards that are jointly achieved. For instance employees who are demanding higher salary will go on strike regardless of their relations to fight for a common course.

vi.   Having the same vision.

vii.   Being of the same status.

viii.   Belonging to same religion.

Brainstorming in groups

This is process aimed at generating a quantity of ideas

It is used to help groups generate multiple ideas and alternative for solving problems. The technique is effective because it helps reduce interference caused by critical and judgmental reactions to one's ideas from other group members

Rules for brainstorming:-

I. Stress quantity over quality: Managers should try to generate and write down as many ideas as possible. Encouraging quantity motivates people to think beyond their petty ideas.

ii. Freewheeling should be encouraged: Managers are advised not to set limit. Group members are advised to offer any and all ideas they have. The wider and more outrageous, the better.

iii. Suspend judgment: Don't criticize during the initial stage of idea generation. Phrases such as "we've never done it that way" "it won't work" "it's too expensive" and "the boss will never agree" should not be used.

iv. Ignore seniority: People are reluctant to freewheel when they are trying to impress the boss or when their ideas are politically motivated. The facilitator of a brainstorming session should emphasize that everyone has the same rank. No one is given veto power when brainstorming.

Teams in Organization

Definition of a team

A team is defined as a group in which the contributions of individuals are seen as complementary (Addair 1986)

Team development stages

Woodcock, in 1979 saw a team as developing through four key stages namely:

1.   Undeveloped team

Contents in this stage include:

i.   Establishment of tasks

ii.   Establishment of rules and regulations

iii.   Acquisition of resources

iv.   Identification of a leader

v.   Formulation of team policy

Experimenting team

Contents

i.   Internal conflicts develops when

ii. Some or all members refuse to perform their tasks

iii. Some members fail to obey their leader

iv. Some members fail to obey their rules and regulations

v. Some members misuse resources.

Consolidating team

Contents

I. Conflict is settled.

ii. Cooperation develops.

iii. Views are exchanged freely.

iv. New standards or norms are developed.\

Mature team

Contents

I. Team work is achieved.

ii. Roles are played in a flexible manner.

iii. Solutions to problems are found.

iv. Solutions to problems are implemented.

Characteristics of effective teams

Effective teams have the following characteristics:

I. Members have clear objectives and agreed goals.

ii. Members support each other.

iii. Members trust each other.

iv.   Members have appropriate leadership.

v.   Members encourage individual group development.

vi.   Members have sound inter group relations.

vii. Members regularly review their progress.

viii.   Members maintain a high degree of cooperation.

ix.   Members are honest to each other.

Team building goals

I. They clarify objectives of the team and the responsibilities of each team member.

ii. They develop team problem solving and decision making objectives

iii. They develop team planning skills.

iv. They determine a preferred style of team work and to change to that style.

v. They fully utilize conceptual skill of each individual member.

vi. They develop open and honest working relationships based on trust and understanding of team members.

CHAPTER SIX

Chapter 6.1 ORGANIZATIONAL CULTURE

Itroduction

Most people do not understand in their own minds what is meant by organizational culture because culture is general concept which is difficult to define or explain precisely.

The concept of culture has developed from anthropology. There is no consensus on culture's meaning or its applications to the analysis of work organization

Definition of culture

    i. Culture is defined as 'how things are done around here'.

A more detailed definition is:

ii. Culture is the collection of traditions, values, policies, beliefs and attitudes that constitute a pervasive context of everything we do and think in an organization.

Levels of culture

i.   Artifact: This is the most visible level of culture and creations of the constructed physical and social environment. It includes physical space and layout, the technology output, written and spoken language and the overt behaviour of group members.

ii.   Values: Cultural learning reflects someone's original values. Solutions about how to deal with new task, issue or problem are based on convictions of reality. If the solutions work, the value can transform into a belief. Values and beliefs, therefore, become part of the conceptual process by which group members justify actions and behaviour.

iii.   Basic underlying assumptions: When a solution to a problem works repeatedly, it comes to be taken for granted. Basic assumptions are unconsciously implicit assumptions that actually guide behavior and determine how group members perceive, think and feel about things.

Types of organizational culture

Organizational culture is classified in different types. Harrison Handy, describes four main types of organizational culture namely:

I. Power culture: This culture depends on a central power source with rays of influence from the central figure throughout the organization. A power culture is frequently found in small entrepreneurial organizations and relies on trust, empathy and personal communications for its effectiveness. Control is exercised from centre by the selection of key individuals. There are few rules and procedures and little bureaucracy. It is a political organization with decisions taken largely on the balance of influence.

ii. Role culture: This culture is often stereotyped as a bureaucracy and works by logic and rationality. Role culture rests on the strength of strong organizational 'pillar'-the functions of specialists in, for example, finance, purchasing and production. The work of, and interaction between, pillars is controlled by procedures and rules and coordinated by the pediment of a small band of senior managers. Role or job description is often more important than the individual and position power is the main source of power.

iii. Task culture: This culture is job oriented or project oriented in terms of structure. The task and culture can be likened to a net, some strands of which are stronger than others and with much of the power and influence at the interstices. An example is the matrix organization. Task culture seeks to bring together the right resources and people and utilize the unifying power of the group. Influence is widely spread and based more on expert power than on position or personal power.

iv. Person culture: This culture is where the individual is the central focus and any structure exists to serve the individuals within it. When a group of people decide that it is in their interests to band together to do their own thing and share office space, equipment or clerical assistance then the resulting organization would have a person culture. Examples are group of barristers, architects, doctors or consultants. Although it is found in only a few organizations, many individuals have a preference for person culture, for example university professors and specialists. Management hierarchies and control mechanisms are possible only by mutual consent. Individuals have almost complete autonomy and any influence over them is likely to be on the basis of personal power.

Influences on the development of culture:

The culture and structure of an organization develop over time and in response to a complex set of factors. Some of the key influences that are likely to play an important roles in the development in any corporate culture include among others:

I. History

Every organization has a history of the founders, founding managers, its duration, the philosophy and values the founding managers established.

If the founding managers established an ambitious philosophy of work, the contemporary managers will be influenced by the set philosophy to work harder so as to maintain status quo.

ii. Goals and objectives

Managers set goals and objectives. They establish a time frame in which they have to achieve them. Managers aggressiveness in their work will be influenced by the set goals and objectives which have to be achieved in the set time frame.

iii. Primary function and technology

The nature of the organization's business and its primary function has an important influence on its culture. This includes the range and quality of products and services provided, the importance of reputation and the type of customers. The primary function of the organization will determine the nature of the technology processes and methods of undertaking work, which in turn also affect structure and culture.

iv. Size

Usually larger organizations have more formalized structure and culture. Increased size is likely to result in separate departments and possibly split-site operation problems. A rapid expansion or decline in size and rate of growth and resultant changes in staffing will influence structure and culture.

v. Location

Geographical location and the physical characteristics of the location in which the organization is located influence the behavior of the customers and employed staff.

The staff and customers in urban locations e.g. busy urban areas tend to have more aggressive culture than those in rural areas.

vi. Management and staffing

Top executives can have considerable influence on the nature of the organization's corporate culture. Top executives who formulate aggressive policies which are favourable to both junior managers and staff will positively influence the corporate culture of the organization.

vii. The environment

In order to be effective, the organization must be responsive to external environmental influence.

For example, if an organization operates in a dynamic environment, it requires a structure and culture that are sensitive and readily adapted to change.

An organic structure is more likely to respond to new opportunities, challenges, risks and limitations represented by external environment.

viii. Heroes

Most people behaviour is influenced by people that have excelled in their operations. Such people will work hard to match the standard of their heroes' great admiration. For example, in football game, upcoming footballers' standard of their play will be influenced by the footballers that have already excelled in football game.

Importance of culture:-

I. Culture helps to account for variations among organizations and manages, both nationally and internationally.

ii. Culture helps to explain why different groups of people perceive things in their own way and perform. things differently from other groups.

iii. Culture can help reduce complexity and uncertainty.

iv. Culture provides a consistency in outlook and values.

v. Culture enables management and staff to easily coordinate their activities.

vi. Culture enables managers to make proper decisions.

vii. Culture enables management and staff to cordially control their operations.

Chapter 6/2: MANAGEMENT OF ORGANIZATIONAL CHANGE

Introduction

Given the complex nature and competitive environment under which modern organizations operate, the way forward for organizations is to adopt strategies, methods and practices which enable them to be ahead of their competitors.

Recent global, political and economic events such as liberalisation of economies, rising cost of production, global economic downturn, the many competing and substitute products in the market and the new spillover effects in the organizations, management are compelled to make decisions so as to remain competitive in the markets.

Definition of organization change

Organizational change can be defined from various perspectives;

Some of the correctly agreed definitions of organization change are:

I. Alteration of existing activity or activities.

ii. 'Innovation', the basic sense of introducing something new in the organization.

iii. Change is fundamentally a learning process that comes about through attempting to resolve task, organizational and human issues (Thukur et al, 1978)

Planned change

Introduction

When an organization makes a conscious effort to change, it is called planned change. In order to bring about a successful change in an individual or organization, certain logical steps needs to be followed.

Steps Of Introducing Change

I. Recognizing the need for change

This seeks to answer the question "is this change necessary?" change should be effected for the sake of change. The rationale for the change must be clearly understood.

ii. Identifying the change method

Several techniques for introducing change to organizations are available. The technique chosen should meet the needs of the organization in reacting to the external environment and the identification of the type of culture that will provide for the greatest productivity in organization.

iii. Unfreezing the status quo

For individuals to change, their present attitudes and beliefs must be altered or unfrozen. Resistance to change must be eliminated or reduced if the change is to be effective. The idea is to create self doubt and provide a means for salvaging/ remedying the situations.

v. Moving to the new situations

The initiation of change can come from an order, recommendation or self directed impetus. However, change is more permanent if a person truly wants and feels a need to change. There should be a two way relationship between the implementers of the change and those being changed.

vi. Refreezing to create a new status quo

Very often changes are introduced do not stick. If change is to stick, those changed must be convinced that it is in their own and organization's best interest. One of the best ways to accomplish this is to collect objective evidence of the success of the change.

Techniques for implementing change:-

Several techniques for implementing planned change are available to managers.

I. The survey feedback method: This is the methods of basing organizational change efforts on the systematic collection and measurement of subordinate attitudes by anonymous questionnaires. The three basic steps in this process are:

·   Data collection.

·   Feedback to organizational units.

·   Action decision.

ii. Team building: A conscious effort to develop effective work groups throughout the organization. These work groups focus on solving actual problems in building efficient management teams. The team building process goes through a series of steps:

- The leader defines a problem that requires organizational change.

- The group analyses the problem to determine the underlying causes.

- The group proposes alternative solutions.

- The group chooses the best alternative.

- The group implements the change.

This helps to ensure support for the change and interpersonal trust and support develops.

iii. Sensitivity training: This Technique uses leaderless discussion groups (also called T-group training or laboratory training). The goal is to develop awareness of and sensitivity to oneself and others. More specifically, the goals of sensitivity training include the following:

- Increased openness with others.

- Greater concern for needs of others.

- Increased tolerance for individual differences.

- Less ethnic/ racial prejudice.

- Awareness and understanding of group processes.

- Enhanced listening skills.

- Greater appreciation on the complexities of behaving competently.

- Establishment of more realistic personal standards of behaviour.

NB: This is not a widely used technique in business organizations today. At times managers are forced to make unpleasant decisions and may therefore be viewed as being insensitive.

iv. Management by Objectives (MbO)

This is a systematic approach that facilitates achievement of results by directing efforts towards attainable goals. MbO encourages managers to plan ahead (for the future) and also encourages participative management approaches. Participation by individuals in setting goals and emphasis on self control promote individuals as well as organizational development.

v. Job Enrichment

Job enrichment refers to the deliberate restructuring of a job to make it more challenging, meaningful and interesting.

vi. The grid approach

This was developed by Robert Blake and Jane Mouton. They suggest that the most effective leadership style is that which stresses maximum concern for both output and people. The grid provides a systematic approach for analyzing the involved data.

vii. Management Development

This involves the efforts to improve the skills and attitudes of present and prospective managers. It also involves learning from more effective ways of managing people and other resources. This programme can be internal or external.

1. External forces of change

These include:-

I. Competitors changing their strategies or other methods of operations.

ii. Economic factors such as poor economic performance may require new cost cutting measures.

iii. Legal forces such as passage of new laws by the government.

iv. Introduction of new type of technology in the market may render the current technology of a firm obsolete.

v. Economic liberalization policy which no longer affords protection of local firms may require them to adopt new methods in production strategies in order to remain competitive in the face of the influx of foreign goods.

vi. Political force such as philosophy of a new government may make people to change their attitude to conform to new philosophy.

vii. Social cultural forces such as changes in societal norms, values and attitudes should be accompanied by corresponding changes in goods and services. For instance, a change in taste requires that a company must change quality levels, features of existing products and services or introduce a completely new product in the market.

viii. Physical forces like change in weather and climatic patterns, for example, adverse weather effects may require a company to adjust its production programme This may be due to shortage of essential agricultural based raw materials.

ix. Demands of trade unions will force management to respond to the demands.

x. Consumers' protection organizations insisting on specific quality standards will force management to be quality sensitive.

Internal forces of change:-

These include:-

i.   Existing procedures which have become irrelevant.

ii.   Existing structures which are too rigid hence the need for flexible ones.

iii. Centralized system of authority which is no longer effective after a major organizational growth and expansion.

iv. Existing technology which may be obsolete.

v.   Existing products and services which are no longer competitive in the market.

vi. Existing training programmes which have become irrelevant in light of changes in work methods and technology.

vii. Existing compensation policy which is not motivational such as automatic salary increment not based on merit. A new compensation method, for example, payment by results (PBR) may need to be introduced.

viii. Negative work attitudes by workers when need to be changed through new policies, rules and procedures.

Resistance to Change

Resistance to change has been associated with change and accepted as a major element of any change process. No matter how change may benefit the organization and individual employees, there will always be a tendency to resist it.

Reasons for resistance to change

i.   Fear of the unknown, for instance, potential difficulties or uncertainties which may come along with a new method or procedure.

ii.   Fear of losing power, prestige or status.

iii.   Failure to understand why a change is being introduced due to poor communication.

iv.   Change can be resisted due to resources limitations i.e. If there are no funds to implement change.

v.   Change is also resisted when group members are very cohesive. They will not want to be separated from each other.

vi.   Cultural beliefs: people will resist change so as to uphold their cultural beliefs.

vii.   Union opposition: labour union representatives often oppose any changes proposed by management if unfavourable to them.

viii.   Limited knowledge: a person will not accept change due to his limited knowledge.

    Techniques of reducing resistance to change:

i.   Educate and communicate effectively with employees on the need and benefits of change.

ii.   Involve employees in planning the change process.

iii.   Negotiate with employees or departments which are likely to resist change.

iv.   Introduce change gradually and provide emotional support including time off during the most difficult period of the change process.

2

v.   Selectively use information which gives emphasis on positive aspects of change.

vi.   Co opt employees likely to resist change.

vii.   Create new positions and assign them to the employees that resist change.

viii. Demand that members accept change or risk losing rewards and other benefits.

ix.   Separate those who completely refuse to change i.e. sack them.

CHAPTER SEVEN

Chapter 7/1: LEADERSHIP

Introduction

Everyone is a leader in all, but name. The essence of leadership is followership. In other words, it is the willingness of the people to follow that makes a person a leader (Koontz, O'Donnel, et al)

Leaders are the creators and "sellers" of culture in the organization. The leader not only creates the national tangible aspects of organizations, such as structure and technology, but is also the creator of symbols, ideologies, languages, beliefs and myths.

Definitions of leadership:

i.   Leadership is the process of influencing others to work willingly towards an organization's goals and to the best of their capabilities. (Koontz, O'Donnell, et al).

ii.   Leadership is the capacity to define oneself to others in a way that clarifies and expands a vision of the future.

Leadership Acceptance

Basis of acceptance:-

I.   Traditional: This leadership is acquired in a monarch and tribal chieftains. For instance, the first born of a monarch becomes a king or queen depending on gender. This is a category to which few people can aspire to. Except in the small family businesses, there are few opportunities for traditional leadership at work.

ii.   Charismatic: This leader gains influence mainly from strength of personality i.e. special talent. Hitler, Churchill, Napoleon, and other leaders that have become great leaders had strong personality. The difficulty with charismatic leadership is that few people possess the exceptional qualities required to transform all around them into willing followers. Another issue is that personal qualities, or traits of leadership cannot be acquired by training, they can only be modified by it.

iii.   Situational: This leader acquires the leadership position for being in the right place at the right time. This kind of leadership is too temporary in nature to be of much value in a business. What is looked for is someone who is capable of assuming a leadership role in a variety of situations over a period of time.

iv.   Legal rational i.e appointed leader: His influence arises directly out of his position, for example, most managers and supervisors assume the leadership roles in this way.

v.   Functional: A functional leader secures his leadership position by what he does rather than by what he is. In other words, a functional leader adapts this behavior to meet the competing needs of the situation.

Qualities of effective leaders

Effective leaders have the following qualities:-

i.   Command of basic facts

ii.   Good personality

iii.   Courageous

iv.   Self discipline

v.   Intelligent

vi.   Social skills

vii.   Ability to inspire others

viii.   Ability to tolerate criticisms

ix.   Willingness to take risk

x.   Relevant professional knowledge

Styles of Leadership

Introduction

The styles of leadership vary from one person to another and from organization to organization depending on the value and personalities of the leaders and on the needs of the organization.

Leaders adopt styles which according to their assessment will achieve effectiveness and efficiency in pursuit of the achievement of organizational goals.

The styles of leadership are:-

i.   Democratic style

ii.   Dictatorial style

iii.   Laissez faire style

iv.   Autocratic style

The enforcement of any one of the styles of leadership is influenced by internal and external forces. A leader keeps on enforcing different styles depending on the nature of the force.

Factors that influence the choice of a leadership style:-

i.   Self knowledge and confidence of the leader.

ii.   Leader's goals and aspirations.

iii.   Academic and professional background of the leader.

iv.   Leader's personality.

v.   Leader's experience.

vi.   Followers skills and experience level.

vii.   Followers academic and professional backgrounds.

viii.   Followers need for independence.

ix.   Followers loyalty to the organization.

x.   Impact of technology.

xi.   Leader-followers relationship.

xii.   Situational stress i.e. time pressure.

xiii.   The culture of the organization.

Leadership styles in practice

1.   Democratic style

Characteristics of a democratic leader

i.   Consults followers.

ii.   Helps followers.

iii.   Socializes with followers.

iv.   Counsels followers.

v.   Punishes after investigation.

vi.   Readily solves problems of the followers.

154

Reactions of the followers to democratic styles:

i.   Maximize production.

ii.   Improve quality of work.

iii.   Health of the followers improves.

iv.   The rate of tardiness decreases.

v.   The percentage of absenteeism decreases.

vi.   The rate of the labour turnover decreases.

vii.   The relationship between the leader and followers improves.

viii.   The relationship among followers improves.

2.   Dictatorial style

Characteristics of a dictatorial leader:

i.   Does not consult followers.

ii.   Does not help followers.

iii.   Is unsocial to followers.

iv.   Does not counsel followers.

v.   Does not solve problems of followers.

Reactions of the followers to dictatorial style:

i.   Poor work output.

ii.   Followers are stressed.

iii.   Followers develop poor health.

iv.   The rate of followers tardiness increases.

v.   The rate of absenteeism increases.

3.   Laissez- faire style

This is a style in which a leader leaves the followers unattended.

Characteristics of a Laissez- faire style leader:

i.   Does not give work to followers.

ii.   Does not consult the followers.

iii.   The leader does not help the followers.

iv.   The leader leaves the followers by themselves.

v.   The leader does not advise the followers.

Reactions of the followers to Laissez-faire style

i.   Followers get stressed.

ii.   The health of followers deteriorates.

iii.   The rate of absenteeism of the followers increases.

iv.   The relationship between followers and the leader worsens due to the leader's failure to give work to followers.

v.   The rate of the labour turns over of the followers increases.

Autocratic style

This style is similar to dictatorial style except that dictators communicate with their followers but do not respond to the followers demands.

Characteristics of an autocratic leader:

i.   Does not consult followers.

ii.   Does not help followers.

iii.   Does not socialize with followers.

iv.   Does not solve problems of followers.

v.   Does not counsel the followers.

Reactions of followers to autocratic style:

i.   Followers have poor work output.

ii.   Followers perform their work poorly.

iii.   Followers' health deteriorates because of poor relations between the leader and followers.

iv.   The rate of the followers' tardiness increases.

v.   The rate of followers' absenteeism increases.

Differences between management and leadership:

Very often, leadership and management are considered as synonymous. Although the definitions of the two terms overlap, there are differences between them. The main differences are:-

diagram

Styles of Management

The styles of management were developed by Rensis Likert. These styles are:

1. Consultative

In this style, the manager consults subordinates when the need arises.

Consultation has the following advantages:

i. Improves relations between the manager and subordinates.

ii. Boosts morale of the subordinates.

iii. Enriches the understanding of the subordinates.

iv. Develops manager's -subordinates degree of cohesiveness.

v. Improves performance of the subordinates in the whole organization, which uplift corporate image of the organization.

vi. Enables the manager to improve his performance.

Disadvantages

i. Consultation gives an impression that the manager does not know. This trend tends to lower degree of respect to the manager

ii.   Consultation wastes time

iii.   The manager, other times, gets wrong advice from the employees.

iv.   When the manager goes to consult, his managerial routine work is interrupted.

v.   Consulting subordinates, manager's capability is lowered.

2.   Participative

This is a management style in which the manager participates in what the employees are doing. In this style, the manager also seeks suggestions and involves employees in decision-making.

Advantages

i.   A manager gets more information about the work.

ii.   Participation improves the relationship between the manager and employees.

iii.   Participation enhances employees job enrichment which lead to improvement of their performance

iv.   Participation enables employees to seek information regarding their work from the manager.

v.   Organizations that encourage managers and employees job participation improve managers and employees degree of cohesiveness.

vi.   The positive results developed by participation between managers and employees uplift corporate image of the organization.

Disadvantages

i.   Participation between the manager and employees make the manager very familiar to employees which lead to down looking upon the manager.

ii.   Participation tends to lower managers skill. Employees perform technical work but managers perform conceptual work.

iii.   When the managers participate in employees work, some employees or all employees have an impression that the manager does not know employees' work operations. This scenario lowers employees respect towards the manager.

iv.   Participation adversely affects managers conceptual work.

v.   Participation fatigues managers.

3.   Benevolent

This is a management style in which a manager gives incentives to employees. Employees that have received incentives relate well with the manager. The production of employees increases.

Advantages

i.   Employees managed using this style maximize production.

ii.   The relations between the manager and employees improve.

iii.   The rate of tardiness of employees declines.

iv.   The rate of absenteeism of employees declines.

v.   There is low rate of labour turnover.

vi.   Uplifts standard of living of employees.

Disadvantages

i.   When the incentives are withdrawn, employees seek better positions elsewhere.

ii.   The relations between management and employees declines.

iii.   When the incentives are withdrawn some employees are involved in fraud i.e embezzlement, forgery and larceny

iv.   Withdrawal of incentives by the management, adversely affects relations between management and employees.

v.   When incentives are withdrawn by the management, some employees leak trade secrets to the competitors.

4.   Authoritative

This is a style in which the manager enforces force to the employees who fail to obey the instructions given by the manager.

Advantages

i.   Employees shall abruptly obey manager's instructions.

ii.   Employees will achieve the target at the required time.

Disadvantages

i.   Enforcement of authoritative style demoralizes employees.

ii.   Enforcement of authoritative style adversely affects the relations between authoritative manager and employees.

iii.   The degree of tardiness of employees increases.

iv.   The rate of absenteeism of employees increases.

v.   The rate of labour turnover increases.

Theories of leadership:-

1.   Trait Theory

A trait is defined as distinctive physical or psychological characteristic of an individual that contributes to his behaviour.

The trait approach to leadership is the evaluation and selection of leaders based on their physical, mental and psychological characteristics.

According to this theory, a successful leader is one who possesses certain traits or qualities. To identify these qualities, research in this area attempted to:

i.   Compare the traits of people who become leaders with those who remain as followers, and

ii.   Identify characteristics and traits possessed by effective leaders.

The study of all successful leaders reveals that they possess similar qualities such as good personality, intelligence, self-confidence, enthusiasm, courage, imagination etc. Some supporters of trait theory believe that leadership qualities are inborn or inherited, while others contend that these traits can be acquired by training and experience.

The key benefit of the trait theory is its simplicity. It is more descriptive than analytical and directs attention to qualities which a person must have in order to become a leader. However, this theory has been criticized on a number of grounds:

The theory examines leadership in isolation and does not consider the leadership environment. Personal traits are only one part of the total environment. Leadership is always related to a particular situation and it is not unusual for a leader to be successful in one situation and unsuccessful in another.

There is no common universal list of traits found in all successful leaders. The qualities and characteristics required by a leader are determined to a large extent by the demands of the situation in which the leader operates.

The theory does not also distinguish between traits which are needed for acquiring leadership and which are necessary for maintaining leadership.

However, the trait approach is not dead, the research is still continuing in this area.

2.   Behaviour theory

This theory is based on the premise that effective leadership is the result of effective role behaviour. Success in leadership depends more on what the leader does than on the traits. The hypothesis is that the behaviour of successful leaders would be different from that of the less successful leaders.

Behaviour theorists attempted to find a set of leader behaviour that would be effective in all leadership situations. What they found was that a certain leader's behavior is more effective in some situations or at some time but not in others. They found that factors other than leader's behaviour moderate leadership effectiveness.

3.   Modern situational theory

According to this theory, the effectiveness of a leader depends upon the situation in which leadership is exercised. The central theme of this theory is that a particular style of leadership may be successful in one situation and unsuccessful in other situations. This approach emphasizes that there is no one best style of leadership universally applicable in all situations. Instead, the leadership process is a function of the leader, the followers and the situation.

A major contribution of the situational theories is that they provide managers with a set of leadership match principles helping managers to select appropriate leadership systems (or behaviours) for particular situations, including:

i.   Know ones leadership style

ii.   Find leadership situations that suit leadership styles

iii.   Change situational factors to suit leadership styles

iv.   Change leadership styles to suit situations.

4.   Path-goal theory of leadership

Path-goal theory of leadership explains that managers can facilitate job performance by showing employees how their performance directly affects their receiving the desired rewards. A manager's behavior contributes to employee satisfaction and acceptance of the manager if it increases goal attainment by employees.

According to this theory, effective job performance results if the manager assists the employee in performing the job effectively and rewards the employee for effective performance i.e clarifies the employee's path to the goal.

5.   Managerial and leadership improvement approaches

Not all people want to lead but some people prefer to follow. It is common in organizations for individuals at one level of management to turn down opportunities for promotion to higher levels.

Most people, however, do enjoy a leadership role and want to improve their leadership ability. Certainly, the inspirational element of leadership is an art, not a science. However, it is evident that many people in the arts, e.g. painting or music, do not improve their skills through education and guided experience.

It follows that managers can bring about some improvement in their leadership abilities through conscientious effort.

Specific approaches that may help include:

i.   Read about leadership.

ii.   Observe those in leadership situations.

iii.   Increase one's knowledge of human behaviour.

iv.   Gain more knowledge of one's field of study.

v.   Improve one's speaking skills.

Chapter 7/2: AUTHORITY

Definition

Authority is defined as the right that an individual has to require a certain action from another or others.

Features of Authority

i.   It is the legitimate right of an individual.

ii.   It is the right to command and control others.

iii.   It is used to achieve organizational goals.

iv.   It may be exercised through persuasions and sanctions.

v.   It is bound to certain limits.

vi.   Authority is the key to the manager's job.

vii.   Authority can be delegated by a manager.

viii.   Authority is the right to influence others .

Types of authority

i.   Formal

A manager will have formal authority when the organization bestows the authority upon the individual by means of his job title and specifying reporting relationships.

ii.   Technical

A manager has technical authority due to his or her special knowledge, personal skills or training. Here, the authority exists only within the scope of that special knowledge, personal skills or training.

iii.   Informal/ personal

This authority is not recognized in any organizational chart. It exists because, without regards to the positions he holds, the person is accepted as being particularly respected, or an elder citizen or is simply popular and recognized by his colleagues as being talented in a particular line of thought.

Centralization and decentralization of authority:

Centralization

This is a process of formulating authority in the same place. When top managers formulate policy in the head office, it is said that the authority has been centralized.

Decentralization

This is a process of formulating authority at different centres, especially in organization's branches.

Factors determining the degree of centralization and decentralization of authority:

i.   Costliness of the decision.

ii.   Desire for uniformity of policy.

iii.   Size and character of the organization .

iv.   History and culture of the organization.

v.   Management philosophy.

vi.   Desire for independence.

vii.   Availability of managers.

viii.   Control techniques.

ix.   Decentralization performance.

x.   Environmental influence.

Advantages of centralization:-

I. Senior management can exercise greater control over the activities of the organization and co-ordinate their subordinates or sub-units more easily.

ii. With central control, procedures can be standardized throughout the organization.

iii. Senior managers can make decisions from the point of view of the organization as a whole, whereas subordinates would tend to make decisions from the point of view of their own department or section.

iv. Centralized control enables an organization to maintain a balance between the different functions or departments. For example, if a company has only a limited amount of funds available to spend over the next few years, centralized management would be able to take a balanced view of how the funds should be shared out.

v.   Senior managers ought to be more experienced and skillful in making decisions. In theory at least, centralized decisions by senior managers should be better in quality than decentralized decisions by less experienced subordinates.

vi. Centralized management will often be cheaper in terms of managerial overheads.

vii. In times of crisis, the organization may need strong leadership by a central group of senior managers.

viii. Centralized decisions are accepted by all staff because they are made by senior management.

ix. Centralization enables senior managers to know what is happening throughout the organization.

Disadvantages of centralization:-

i.   Increases stress and burdens senior management.

ii.   Deprives subordinates of job satisfaction and more so in decision making which affects their work.

iii. Senior managers do not have better knowledge of local conditions affecting subordinates' work.

iv. Subordinates in centralized organizations are denied the chance to prepare for senior positions.

v.   Centralizing authority enhances the possibility of top management misuse of power.

vi. Centralizing authority adversely affects the relationship between management and subordinates.

Advantages of decentralization:-

i.   It reduces stress and burdens of senior management.

ii.   It provides subordinates with greater job satisfaction by giving them more say in decision making which affects their work.

iii.   Subordinates may have a greater knowledge of local conditions affecting their area of work.

iv.   Decentralization allows greater flexibility, a quicker response to changing conditions and quicker decision making.

v.   By allowing delegated authority to subordinates, management at middle and junior levels are groomed for eventual senior management positions, because they are given the necessary experience of decision making.

vi.   By establishing appropriate sub-units or profit centers to which authority is delegated, the system of control within the organization might actually be improved.

vii.   By decentralizing authority, it reduces the possibility of top management misuse f power.

viii.   Decentralization improves relations between management and subordinates.

Disadvantages of decentralization

i.   Senior management are denied the possibility of controlling activities of the organization.

ii.   Decentralization of authority undermines the standardization of procedures throughout the organization.

iii.   Senior management are not able to maintain a balance between different functions or departments.

iv.   Subordinate managers' decisions are likely to be of low quality because they are less qualified and experienced.

v.   Senior management is deprived of the right to make decisions from the point of view of the whole organization.

vi.   Decentralized operations are often expensive in terms of management overheads.

vii.   Senior managers will not know what is happening throughout the organization.

viii.   Decentralized decisions tend to be ignored by subordinates because they are not made by senior management.

Importance of authority:-

I. Authority makes things happen in organizations.

ii. Authority enables managers to achieve goals of the organization.

iii. Authority is important to the supervisors because it enables them to achieve their supervisory roles.

iv. Authority enables managers in the organization to execute their responsibilities.

v. People obey individuals in authority not because they like or respect them but because of the rights outlined in their positions.

vi. Authority enables the managers to give orders which must be obeyed.

Chapter 7/3: POWER

Introduction

Power is a useful concept with which to explain why different people exert different degrees of influence. As with leadership, power is a property of the relationship between the more and less powerful. The exercise of power is therefore a social process.

Power is a critical dimension of leadership and the two terms are often used with the same or similar meanings.

Definition

Power is the ability of an individual to control or to influence another or others to do something.

Sources of Power:-

i.   Reward power

A leader has reward power if the followers believe that the leader is able to control rewards that they value, and that the leader will part with these rewards in return for compliance with instructions.

In organization the rewards may include promotions, recognition for good performance and many other benefits.

ii.   Coercive power

A leader has coercive power if followers believe that the leader is able and willing to administrator penalties that they dislike.

In organizations, these penalties may include demotion, dismissal etc. Followers will therefore obey the leader to avoid the enforcement of these penalties.

iii.   Hidden power

A manager has a hidden power if he hides information and demands a reward of any form so as to reveal the information.

A person will therefore surrender the reward to have the information revealed.

iv.   Referent power

A leader has referent power if followers believe that the leader has characteristics that are desirable and that they should copy. Followers will thus identify themselves with the leader, regardless of what he actually does.

v.   Charismatic power

This power originates from a leader due to his special talent that followers do not have. Followers will obey the leader so as to benefit from the leader's special talent. The special talent may include wisdom, special knowledge etc.

vi.   Physique power

This power originates from the person due to his body stature. Big bodied people tend to be more influential than small bodied ones.

vii.   Expert power

A leader has expert power if followers believe that the leader has superior knowledge and expertise which is relevant to the particular tasks or activities in hand. To enforce the power, the leader has to demonstrate relevant ability.

viii.   Legitimate / position power

A leader has legitimate/ position power if followers believe that the leader has a right to give them orders which they, in turn have to accept.

Followers will obey the leader to escape enforcement of punishment.

ix.   Dependency

This is power in which a person depends on another for example a wife or husband depending fully on the other.

x.   Connection power

This power is based on the user's relationship with influential people. One relies on the use of contacts or friends who can influence the person one is dealing with. The right connections can give power or at least the perception power. If people know that one is friendly with people in power, they are more likely to do as one requests.

xi.   Information power

Information power is based on others needs for data. Managers rely on information which is usually, but not always, related to the job. Some assistants have more information and are more helpful in answering questions than the managers they work for. An important part of manager's job is to convey information. Employees often go to managers for information on what to do and how to do it.

CHAPTER EIGHT

Chapter 8/1 MOTIVATION

Introduction

The main aim of researchers in management was to establish how managers would achieve effectiveness and efficiency in their work.

To enable themselves become effective and efficient, they grouped themselves into:

i.   Scientific and classical

ii.   Behavioural / human relations

iii.   Systems and contingency

i.   Scientific and classical group felt that they would motivate the people by enabling them to use fully the scientific tools. They also felt that motivation would also be derived from effective and efficient enforcement of the principles of management namely; forecasting, planning, directing, organizing, controlling and coordination.

ii.   Behavioural/ human relations group felt that they would motivate people by paying them better salaries/ wages, improved staff services and enabling each employee to use fully his talent.

iii.   Systems and contingency group felt that the aim would be achieved by coordinating the operations of the organization's departments and also coordination of staff operations. Because forces that demotivate people exist within the environment, managers have continued developing concepts which motivate people.

Definitions of Motivation

I. Motivation is a decision making process through which an individual chooses a desired outcome and sets in motion behavior appropriate to acquiring it

ii. Motivation is a process of influencing employees to act, so that the goals of the organization can be achieved and the needs of the employees be satisfied.

Motivational Theories:-

Motivational theories are focused on psychological factors namely;

1.   Content Theories

These theories concentrate on what motivates people by attempting to develop an understanding of fundamental human needs.

2.   Process Theories

These theories are more concerned with how motivation is aroused and maintained.

Types of Content Theories:-

1. Managerial needs theory

This theory was developed by Mclelland in 1961. He conducted research with over 500 managers from 25 different US corporations to determine just what motivates a good manager. Upon the basis of this research, he argues that managers posses three basic motivational needs namely affiliation, achievement and power.

Importantly, each of these three levels of needs has been linked to both job satisfaction and competence in a number of occupations particularly management. (Medcof and Hausdorf, 1995)

i. Need for affiliation (N – Aff)

This is the desire for friendly, close interpersonal relationship and conflict avoidance.

People with the need for affiliation seek companionship, social approval and satisfying   interpersonal relationships.

People with the need for affiliation display the following characteristics:

.   Take interest in work that provides companionship and social approval.

.   Prefer cooperative situations than competitive ones.

.   Desire relationships involving a high degree of mutual understanding.

.   Strive for approval from both their subordinates and superiors.

.   Expend a lot of energy on maintaining relationships at the expense of getting the job done.

People who fall in the need for affiliation are those who are likely to have developed in an environment which :

. was non-competitive

. was friendly

ii.   Need for achievement (N-Ach)

According to Mclelland, the need for achievement or desire to do something better or more efficiently than it has been done before, is one of the keys of economic growth.

High achievers often exhibit the following behaviour :

i.   Seek personal responsibility for finding solutions to problems.

ii.   Want prompt feedback on their performance to ascertain how they have performed.

iii.   Positively enjoy competition.

iv.   Like to set, strive for and reach difficult goals.

v.   Like to take calculated risks.

vi.   Work hard until they attain excellence.

Mclelland suggested that people high on this motivate are likely to have grown up in environment which:

I. Expected competence of them.

ii. Gave them independence at an early age.

iii. Evaluated them highly.

iii.   Need for power (N- Pow)

This is the desire to cause others behave in a way that they would not have behaved in, if they were left to make their own decision.

Individuals with high need for power often exhibit the following behaviour:

I. Enjoy being in charge.

ii. Like to influence others.

iii. Prefer to be placed in competitive situations.

iv. Forcefully express opinions.

v. Have interest in persuasions.

vi. Have a high degree of self control.

Mclelland suggested that people high on this need are likely to have grown up in environment which:

I. Had a powerful personality.

ii. Had uncompromising leaders.

2. Maslow theory hierarchy of needs

The first comprehensive attempt to classify human needs (motivates) and develop a universal motivational theory was that of Abraham Maslow (1942).

Maslow proposed that human needs can be classified into motivating factors that influence people's behavior which he described as hierarchy of needs.

Maslow postulated that people have several areas of needs, each of which needs to be satisfied before other needs become predominant. Once satisfied, a previous need is no longer a motivator.

Maslow classified needs into five hierarchies

(See the diagram below)

diagram

Diagram: Maslow's Theory hierarchy of needs (Source: Maslow 1942)

Level 1 Physiological needs

These needs include hunger, thirst, clothing, air, sex etc; must be satisfied first.

Level 2 Safety and security needs

Once physiological needs are satisfied, people turn their attention on safety and security needs such as providing a shelter to protect themselves from the enemies or other dangers.

Level 3   Belonging/social needs

The belonging/ social level relates to satisfying social needs, for example by belonging to a group.

Level 4 Self esteem needs

Once belonging and social needs are met, they are replaced with a need for self esteem, such as the desire for high status within a peer group, for example feeling useful, valued, important, respected, worth.

Level 5 Self actualization/fulfillment needs

The need for self actualization/ fulfillment level resides at the top of the hierarchy. It refers to the need for a person to fulfill this potential.

Such needs can be satisfied through:

i.   Business

ii.   Politics

iii.   Religion

iv.   Sports

v.   Music

The satisfaction of these needs may lead to the realization of:

i.   Glory

ii.   Achievement

iii.   Power

iv.   Fame

Note:- The basic needs must be satisfied before the rest level of needs becomes important. For example, social needs become important only after perceived safety and security has been met. When a person level of needs is adequately satisfied, it ceases to dominate and influence behaviour. The next level of needs then becomes the important motivating factor.

Critical analysis of Maslow theory hierarchy needs:

Although all five needs are claimed to exist within everyone, they are, however not uniformly motivating.

I.   At any given moment, different people are likely to be striving to fulfill different need levels of the hierarchy. For example, an individual whose belonging and social needs are dominant (level 3), is likely to behave differently to someone attempting to satisfy safety and security needs (level 2). This presents a problem for managers in that, if each worker has a different hierarchy of needs, how does a manager provide motivators for all his staff?

ii.   The simplicity of the hierarchy does not reflect the reality that the behaviour in the real sense is shaped by situational pressure and controls that are often beyond a person's individual control. As such, it does not recognize that people behaviour can only be fully understood by examining the reciprocal relationship between person, behavioural and situational characteristics.

iii.   The model assumes that one motive should predominate at any moment in time. However, humans are more complex than this. For example, people work to simultaneously attain pay and rewards (security), social contact (belongings), status (self esteem) etc.

iv.   The hierarchy is difficult to relate to work processes, because people do not necessarily satisfy their higher order needs through their jobs or occupations. . Most people prefer to satisfy their needs outside the work place, for example through leisure activities.

v.   The five needs are not defined with sufficient precision, making it difficult, if not impossible, for a manager to make use of the hierarchy to address problems of mass absenteeism every Monday morning.

3. Two Factors Theory

This theory was developed by Fredrick Herzberg.

Fredrick Herzberg, in his book 'work and the nature of man' identified the elements which cause job dissatisfaction and those which can cause job satisfaction. He distinguished them by naming them.

I. Hygiene Factors Theory

This theory contains factors that cause dissatisfaction at work:-

These factors are;

i.   Company policy

ii.   Administration

iii.   Salary/ wage

iv.   The quality of supervision

v.   Interpersonal relations

vi.   Working conditions

vii.   Job security

When people are dissatisfied with their work, it is usually because of discontent with the environmental factors. Herzberg calls such factors "hygiene "factors, hygiene because they are essentially preventive. They prevent or minimize threats to health but do not give good health.

The important concept is that motivation through the above mentioned factors is a necessary but thankless task. It is never ending. Even if it is effective, it will not motivate the employee to work well (at a higher than usual level of performance) except for a short period of time.

On the other hand, if the environment is deficient in some way then the subordinates are likely to become annoyed and to show their displeasure by industrial conflict, decreased productivity, grumbling etc. yet, if the deficiency is corrected, the best that can be expected is that the effort will return to normal.

ii. Motivator Factors Theory

Motivator factors create job satisfaction and are effective in motivating an individual to superior performance and effort. These factors give the individual a sense of self fulfillment or personal growth and consist of:-

i.   Status

ii.   Advancement

iii.   Gaining recognition

iv.   Challenging work

v.   Achievement

vi.   Growth in the job

4.   ERG Theory

Existence, Relatedness and Growth theory (ERG) is built upon Maslow hierarchy of needs theory.

It collapses Maslow's five levels of needs into three categories namely:-

I. Existence needs:

Are desires for satisfying interpersonal relationships. In terms of Maslow's model, existence needs include physiological and safety needs.

ii. Relatedness Needs:

Are desires for satisfying interpersonal relationships. In terms of Maslow's needs, relatedness corresponds to sexual needs.

iii. Growth Needs:

Are desires for continued psychological growth and development. In terms of Maslow's model, growth need include self actualization and esteem needs.

5. Path goal theory of motivation

Path goal theory is the proposition that managers can facilitate job performance by showing employees how their performance directly affects their receiving the desired rewards. A manager's behavior causes or contributes to employee satisfaction and acceptance of the manager if it increases goal attainment by employees.

According to this theory, effective job performance results if the manager assists the employee in performing the job effectively and rewards the employees for effective performance (i.e it clarifies employees path to the goal).

Four distinct leadership / management behaviours are associated with this theory:

i.   Directive: The manager tells the subordinate what to do, and when to do it. There is no employee participation in decision making.

ii.   Supportive: The manager is friendly and shows interest in employees.

iii.   Participative: The manager seeks suggestions and involves employees in decision making.

iv.   Achievement oriented: The manager establishes challenging goals and demonstrates confidence in employees in achieving these goals.

Goals should be set at challenging but realistic level. Difficult goals lead to better performance. Managers are advised to set achievable goals because workers will be demotivated when they fail to achieve target.

1. Process Theories

These theories are more concerned with how motivation is aroused and maintained.

Types of process theory:

1.   The expectancy theory of motivation

This theory states that the strength of an individual's motivation to do something will depend on the extent to which he expects the result of his efforts, if successfully achieved, will contribute towards his own personal needs or goals.

Victor Vroom, suggested that the strength of an individual's motivation to behave in a certain way is a product of two factors:

i.   The strength of his preferences for a certain outcome, vroom called this 'valence'.

ii.   His expectancy that the outcome will result from the intended mode of behavior, thus vroom valence – expectancy theory is that:-

diagram

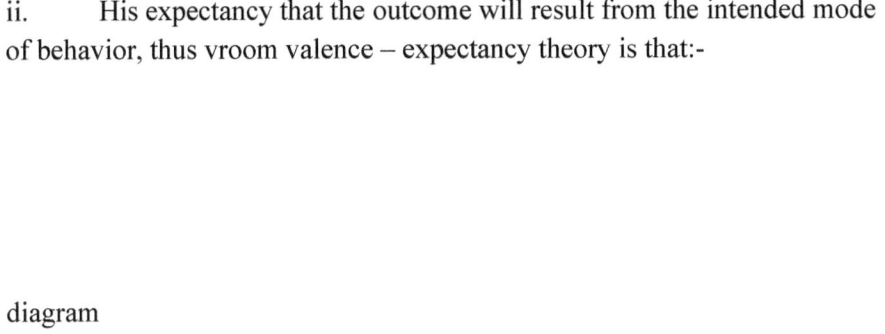

For example an individual might want promotion or an increase in pay. The strength of his desire is his promotion or pay valence. If he has a strong expectancy that harder work will result in promotion or an increase in pay, he will be strongly motivated to work harder. On the other hand, if the individual is not concerned with promotion (i.e the valence is negative) he will not be motivated to do anything which might secure him a promotion; indeed, he might act to prevent such a possibility from arising.

3.   Equity Theory (Stacy Adams)

This theory states that people are happiest in relationships where they give and take equally.

If a person is getting too little from a relationship, then he/ she is likely to be unhappy and the person getting a bigger share may feel guilty about the imbalance.

This scenario is reinforced by strong social norms about fairness.

Equity theory looks at an individual's perceived fairness of an employment situation and finds that perceived inequalities can lead to changes in behaviour.

When people believe that they are treated unfairly in comparison with their co-workers, they will react in one or five ways:-

i.   Reduce their work inputs to match the rewards they are receiving.

ii.   Ask for fair treatment.

iii.   Take legal action.

iv.   Change their own perception of the situation.

v.   Feel guilty.

3.   Drivers Theory (Kahler)

Kahler identified five common drivers that motivate us and which can be at the root of dysfunctional behaviours. These are commonly known as transactional analysis drivers although they can be individually used or stand alone.

These drivers are:-

i.   Being perfect

ii.   Being strong

iii.   Hang up

iv.   Please others

v.   Try hard

4.   Goals setting theory

Introduction

The goal of every organization is to survive, develop, grow and make profit.

Most managers motivate their staff to achieve the set goals or targets. They write vision statements and set deadlines.

Goal setting theory became popular when Locke and Latham carried a research in 1990 to establish whether goal focused people achieved the set goals as planned. The research revealed that when workers are organized and motivated to achieve a set objective, they normally achieve it.

Definition

Goal setting theory states that if a goal is related to specific tasks requirements and is accepted by employees, virtually any type of action that is able to be measured and controlled can be improved.

Basic principles of goal setting theory:-

i.   People goals or intentions play an important part in determining behaviour.

ii.   People do strive to achieve goals in order to satisfy their emotions and desires.

iii.   Goals guide people's responses and actions.

iv.   Goals also direct the work behaviour and performances.

v.   Goals lead to consequences or feedback.

vi.   Goals should be set at challenging but realistic level.

vii.   Difficulty goals lead to higher performance, however, if the set goals are too high or impossible to achieve, the performance will suffer or be affected over a long period.

viii. Specific performance goals should be set in order to direct behaviour and maintain motivation.

ix.   Complete, accurate and timely feedback and knowledge of results is usually associated with high performance.

x.   Feedback provides a means of checking progress on the goals attainment.

xi.   Goals can be determined either by a superior or by the juniors themselves.

xii.   Goals which are set by a superior and juniors' participation lead to high performance.

5. Carrot and Stick Theory

This theory relates to the use of rewards and penalties in order to induce the desired behaviour.

'Carrot' refers to money inform of pay or other financial incentives, such as, allowances, bonuses etc.

'Stick' in form of fear, for example loss of job, income, withdrawal of fringe benefits, demotions etc will motivate people to work harder to avoid the enforcement of them.

Carrot and Stick theory has continued to be a strong motivator. Managers are, however, advised to apply it carefully because it can cause conflict especially when the stick aspect is enforced.

6.   Theory X and Y

Theory X and Y were developed by Douglas McGregor.

i. Theory X

· This theory states that an average person has an inherent dislike of work and will avoid it if he can.

· Because of this human characteristic of dislike of work, most people must be:-

.   Coerced

.   Controlled

.   Directed

. Threatened with punishment to get them to put forth adequate effort towards achievement of organization objectives.

· And also wishes an average person An average person prefers to be directed, wish to avoid responsibility.

· An average person also wants security above all

· The most significant reward that can be offered to an average person in order to obtain commitment is the satisfaction of the individual's actualizing needs.

· The average human being learns, under proper conditions, not only to accept but to seek responsibility.

· Theory X stresses domination and dependence in work relationship.

· Theory X supervision, when the rules are properly applied, should be successful in achieving stated objectives.

ii. Theory Y

This theory states that human beings like working. They equate work to playing or resting

A theory Y manager operates on the basis of vastly different assumptions, believing that effective organizational climate has looser, more general supervision, greater decentralization of authority, less reliance on coercion and control, a democratic style of leadership and greater participation in decision making. The assumptions on which this type of organizational climate is based are:-

I. Work is as natural as play or rest and therefore not avoided.

ii. Self motivation and inherent satisfaction in work will be forthcoming in situations where the individual is committed to organizational goals. That coercion is not the only form of influence that can be used to motivate.

iii. Commitment is a crucial factor in motivation and is a function of the rewards coming from it.

iv. Average individuals learn to accept and even to seek responsibility, given the proper environment.

v. Contrary to stereotypes, ability to be creative and innovative in the solution of an organization's problems is widely, not narrowly, distributed in the population.

vi. In modern organizations, human intellectual potentialities are just partially realized.

McGregor presented these two theories as alternatives and yet, undoubtedly, McGregor himself believed whole heartedly in Theory Y.

There is impressive evidence for theory Y. In most jobs, most workers, even those hostile to bosses and organization, want to like their work and look for achievement. In most jobs even the most alienated workers manage to find something that gives them satisfaction. Studies which were later undertaken on the two theories found out that theory Y is not by itself adequate. This brought a lot of criticism of Abraham Maslow and Warren Bennis.

Theory Z

Theory Z was put forward by W G Ouchi as an 'advance' on theory Y. It attempts to draw on the successful management techniques of large Japanese companies, and suggests how the key elements of successful Japanese management methods can be applied to Western management and organization.

To understand theory Z, it will be helpful to know something about the characteristics of large Japanese firms.

I.   Large firms are able to provide lifetime employment for their employees who are expected in return to be dedicated 'company men'. Lifetime employment gives employees greater career stability, and tends to contribute to better industrial relations.

ii.   For a large part of their career, employees retain the same job status and pay, and are not promoted. Only employees with sufficient seniority (typically, half way through their career) become eligible for promotion. Since young managers cannot expect to be rewarded for good short term performances, there is less incentive to work for short term results at the expense of longer- term benefits. Inter- departmental disputes are less likely to arise and co-operation between managers is more easily achievable in the absence of 'political' in fighting.

iii.   Large firms spend large amounts of money on the welfare of their employees – housing, sports and social facilities, and medical care as well as training.

Broadly speaking, large Japanese firms are characterized by co-operation between management and employees and between managers and departments. Decisions are usually reached by consensus, rather than by a senior manager taking a decision and selling it or imposing it on his subordinates.

Theory Z is based on the belief that it is the spirit of co-operation, and the consensus approach to decision making, that gives Japanese firms the advantages of higher employee motivation, better productivity and higher output quality. Theory Z therefore argues that:-

i.   Although individual managers might have to accept responsibility for decisions, there should be a consensus in decision making, reached by agreement with the manager's subordinates and colleagues. In Japan, the concept of collective responsibility is sometimes used.

ii.   Although there is a formal organization and management hierarchy, decisions are nevertheless democratic and based on trust between managers and subordinates.

iii.   This participative approach to decision making encourages the free flow of information between departments as well as between managers and subordinates.

iv.   Work activities should be 'humanised'. Individual employees are not simply regarded as a functional cog in the wheel.

For consensus decision making to work and for an atmosphere of trust to develop between managers and subordinates, there must be an erosion of status consciousness. Separate canteens of managers and workers cannot be permitted and managers should really dress in the same way as workers, in standard type overalls. Employees must also be rewarded for their commitment to the firm, but not in such a way that the desire for rewards affects what they think and do to secure lifetime employment is a more effective reward than early promotion.

Theory Z is thus an extension of theory Y, with the participative approach to decision-making emphasized as a need for consensus, and with an emphasis on personal commitment and the humanization of work activities.

Motivators

The following are some of the methods of improving motivation:

i.   Pay as a motivator

A view held by many managers is that employees can be motivated to do their work more quickly and efficiently if they are given the incentive of higher pay for better effort.

Incentive schemes may take a variety of different forms such as:

1   Piece work: By this methods, employees are paid a stated amount for each unit or piece of work they do. In many cases, employees receive a basic wage, plus a bonus calculated on piece work principles. This method is often applied to sales personnel, based on sales they obtain.

2   A high day -rate system: Some employees are paid a high hourly rate of pay, with the intention that top quality individuals will apply for the jobs and high rates of pay will stimulate them to work well.

3   A profit sharing plan: This is a method whereby all employees receive an end year bonus (possibly in the form of shares in the company) based on the profits for the company.

ii.   Suggestions Schemes

Employees get motivated when they are asked by management to give their suggestions regarding the work operation.

iii.   Joint- consultative committee

Inviting employees and their representatives to hold meetings with management representatives motivate employees because in such meetings, they highlight their opinions regarding the work.

iv.   Job rotation

Working on the same desk and performing the same operations lowers employees morale. Rotated employees perform variety of operations which motivate them.

v.   Job enrichment

An employee, who is assigned a senior operation to perform it together with his operations, will be motivated by the assigned senior operation.

vi.   Training of staff

Training staff motivates them because, staff acquire more knowledge and skill. The acquired knowledge and skill give them hope of promotion which enhances their motivation.

vii.   Job enlargement

Job enlargement is the attempt to widen a job by increasing the number of operations in which a job holder is involved. This has the effect of strengthening the time cycle or repeated operations of the same work, the dullness of the job reduces leading to the motivation employees.

viii.   Job security

Employees production increases when they work in a secure environment.

ix.   Company policy

Employees that are involved in formulation of company policy have a higher degree of motivation than those not involved in the formulation of policy.

CHAPTER 9

Chapter 9/1 MANAGEMENT DEVELOPMENT

Introduction

In the field of training and development, management development has become an important activity in its own right. It has developed its own technique, practices and literature.

Definition

Management development is a continuous improvement of effectiveness within a particular system, which may be a person, but in the case of management development is within the management function of the organization (Morris, 1978).

Management development Methods:-

i.   Management Education

Qualification – bearing courses run by universities or public sector colleges, for example Mba degrees, diploma in management studies (DMS) and various professional examinations, such as the Kenya Institute of Management (Diploma in Business management), the level of work regarded as post experience and the emphasis is not acquiring theory and empirical knowledge.

ii.   Management Training

Internal and external courses, of the job and focusing on acquiring specific knowledge and relevant job skills. Includes experiental learning and course exercises.

iii.   Experiential Learning

Learning by doing, on the job experience usually with guidance from superiors or colleagues.

Methods of experiential approaches to management development:

1   Coaching/ Guided Experience

This method is planned in such a way that involves the manager in advising and aiding subordinate managers to develop effective job performance. It also involves discovery learning with support.

Advantages:-

i.   It is relevant to the leaner.

ii.   Improves collaboration between parties.

iii.   Good feedback for junior managers.

iv.   Junior managers develop a higher degree of confidence.

v.   Junior managers develop results centered mind.

2   Projects

A specific problem or opportunity is worked on by an individual or a team with the objective of producing concrete results in a given time span.

Advantages:-

i.   May generate a high degree of commitment.

ii.   Utilizes problem –solving methods.

iii.   Improves negotiating skills.

iv.   It builds confidence of individuals participating in this method.

3   Secondments

In this method, a manager is assigned to a post in another department or unit for a limited period.

Advantages:-

i.   Manager acquires valuable experience based on the job.

ii.   Enable the manager to know other people.

iii.   Enables the manager to know other people.

iv.   Builds the confidence of seconded manager.

v.   The exposure enables manager to learn new ideas which improve his job.

4   Experiential Methods (Courses)

Typical methods used in these courses are described briefly in the figure A below.

METHOD   SALIENT FEATURES
             ADVANTAGE

Group exercise   Group given a task and certain limits,
             Definable focus activities; task

                        the results achieved and the process by
             provides peg on which discussion

                        which they were achieved are examined   can
take place; useful for

by the group and a tutor.
leadership and team building.

Role playing   Individuals take on a role and experience
          Participants learn to think on their

                    the nature of an interpersonal encounter,
          feet; experience genuine emotions

                    may be tightly or loosely scripted.
          so long as role is authentic.

Sensitivity training   Group exercises in which processes taking
          Enable groups to explore

                    place in the group are examined; the focus
          interpersonal relations and to

                    is on the 'here and now' interactions; require
          share feelings

careful guidance by trainer.

Case study   A real or imaginary account of an
          Provides focal point developing

                    organizational problem is studied
          analytical and problem solving

by an individual or a small group with

skills.

a view to diagnosing a situation or

proposing solutions.

Brainstorming   A group is asked to suggest ways of   Has proved to be an effective

dealing with an issue/ problem; no
means of stimulating new ideas

discussion or criticism of suggestion   and creating suggestions.

is made until after the list has been

completed.

Simulation exercise   This is a combination of a case study   As a kind of enlarged role play,

with role play; participants are given   this
can reproduce many real life

a fairly detailed scenario and are asked
situations, useful for developing

to undertake a number of decisions
negotiating and decision making

within a time limit.
skills.

Workshops   These are practical exercises in which
Provide opportunity to share ideas

                     participants work on a particular work-   or
real day to day problems, useful

                     based problems as a group.
when devising plans/systems.

Figure A experiential methods (courses).

Succession planning

One of the key features of a structure of management development system is a succession plan. This is basically a plan for identifying who is currently in post and who is available and qualified to take over in the event of retirement, voluntary leaving, dismissal or sickness for example as the figure B below indicates, a typical succession chart includes details of key management job holders and brief references to their possible succession.

diagram

Management development audit

To ensure that the provision adopted by any organization for developing its managers do produce the intended results. The essence of the audit approach is to ask individual managers to describe their own experience and views about management development and then to reflect the collective view back to those responsible for making decisions about the development of managers.

Management development and corporate culture

The approach to management development in an organization will tend to reflect the dominant value system of the senior management. They are persons who, above all, are charged with building a management team and developing their successors. If the top management is centralist and bureaucratic, for example, then its view of management development is likely to produce a logically structured systems such as that shown in figure C below. In such a system, job descriptions, appraisal forms, succession charts and the like are vital items in the analysis of needs and in decisions about how they are to be met. Such a system would probably favour structured efforts, both on and off the job to supply individual manager needs when top management development is on self development on the job. Where management is considered an elite group, then features such as accelerated promotion and graduate trainee programmes tend to predominate. Such systems provide selective support for manager development by concentrating on so called 'high fliers' i.e persons with outstanding potential.

\

Formal management development system

Corporate plan

Future needs

Organization Culture   Management manpower

review

Present Needs   Management manpower
Succession planning requirements   Potential performance

Recruitment   Performance appraisal

Present Performance   Training development activities Off the
job

On the job   Evaluation review

Management development audit

Figure c

Conclusion

The current mood among writers and researchers on management development suggests that a contingency approach to management development is preferable. A contingency approach in essence adapts to the dominant culture of the organization concerned, both takes into account a number of forces for change, such as the influence of new technology. The most successful attempts at management development are likely to be those relying on an appropriate mix of on- the -job experience and off -job courses offered in a variety of ways to meet different individual requirements and learning styles.

Chapter 9/2: CONCEPTS OF EFFECTIVE AND EFFICIENCY ORGANIZATION

Introduction

The main goal of every organization is to achieve the intended goal in a harmonious environment.

Organizations need to be efficient and effective in doing the right things, in the optimum use of their resources. Performance should be related t such factors as increasing profitability and improved service delivery.

Factors influencing effectiveness and efficiency

1.   Ability of the manager e.g.

i.   Strong Personality

A manager must have a strong personality. Managers with weak personality are not able to mobilize workers towards achieving the goal.

ii.   Positive Attitude

Most managers fail because of having negative attitude in what they do. Negative attitudes lower the effectiveness of the manager leading to the failure of achieving the intended goal.

iii.   Relevant Training

For a manager to succeed, one should have relevant training. Most managers fail to achieve their goals because of being placed on desks in which functions are completely irrelevant to their training

iv.   Relevant Experience

Some managers are placed on jobs that they have little or no experience at all. Relevant experience is the best for managers and therefore managers should perform jobs relevant to their training.

v.   Ideal Age

After training which is conducted after education, the manager's age is usually low. Very young managers find it hard to manage elderly workers. Managers, therefore, are supposed to have ideal age, perhaps over twenty five years to be able to effectively manage.

2.   Economic Environment

i.   Fair Competition

For a manager to achieve effectiveness in his work, he is expected to work in an environment in which competition is fairly enforced. A manager cannot achieve effectiveness in environment in which competition is unfairly enforced.

ii.   Strong Economy

A manager working in an environment that enjoys strong economy is able to achieve his goal at the expected time frame.

iii.   Availability of Resources

It is possible for a manager to achieve effectiveness if one does not have necessary resources. To achieve effectiveness, a manager is liable to have the necessary resources at his disposal.

iv.   Ideal Capacity

Limited capacity causes effective managers fail to achieve their goals because they are not able to perform beyond the limited space.

3.   Physical Environment

i)   Ideal Location

For a manager to succeed, he is supposed to work in an organization which is located in an ideal place. For example Nairobi city is ideal location because managers are easily able to get in touch with north, east, west and south (NEWS). Therefore managers in Nairobi and other locations well placed easily achieve their goals.

ii)   Availability of Amenities

Amenities such as recreation facilities, playgrounds are necessary. After work, managers need to take part in games and other leisure activities to reduce their stress. Stress lowers manager's effectiveness.

iii)   Safety

Managers that operate in secure environment concentrate in their work which leads to the achievement of effectiveness and efficiency.

iv)   Ideal climate

Managers and employees that operate in climates that are not favourable are not able to achieve effectiveness and efficiency.

v)   Ideal layout

For a business to succeed, the manager and employees are supposed to work in business which is in an ideal space.

4.   Group Relations

i)   The span of control should be reasonable. Large groups find it hard to achieve their goals.

ii)   Ideal age of group members

Group members are expected to be of a reasonable age. Very young people are likely not to be cohesive which will make them not achieve effectiveness and efficiency.

iii)   Achievable goals

Managers are advised to set achievable goals. Very ambitious goals overwork employees which adversely affect the achievement of their effectiveness and efficiency.

iv)   Effective leader

Some leaders are not effective and therefore cannot achieve effectiveness. Management is required to employ effective leaders/managers who are able to improve group cohesiveness.

v)   Managers should allocate understandable tasks. Very difficult tasks stress workers which lead to the failure of achieving effectiveness and efficiency.

5.   Leadership

i)   To achieve effectiveness, managers must have relevant knowledge and skills.

ii)   Managers/leaders should be able to enforce the right leadership styles in different situations.

iii)   Managers are supposed to set right standards i.e the standards that can easily be achieved.

iv)   Managers /leaders should establish strong power base.

v)   To achieve effectiveness, managers should allocate understandable tasks.

6.   Systems and Structures

So as to achieve effectiveness and efficiency, managers/leaders should establish:-

i)   Efficient administrative structure.

ii)   Fair control system.

iii)   Ideal reward system.

iv)   Strong power base - this can be achieved by treating all members of staff impartially.

v)   Strong team work.

7.   Motivation to work

i.   Workers should be promoted fairly i.e due to their ideal qualifications and experience.

ii.   Employees that perform excellently well should be accordingly rewarded.

iii.   All staff should be trained if the management expects to achieve effectiveness.

iv.   Managers and workers should be allocated good offices with all required facilities.

v.   Employees should be paid better salaries so as to motivate them to work harder.

8.   Technology environment

i)   Current and efficient technology should be introduced in the organization to enable the manager achieve efficiency.

ii)   There should be qualified technicians to repair the equipment promptly when it needs to be repaired.

iii)   Equipment should be durable.

iv)   Equipment should have high resale value.

v)   Equipment should have low depreciation rate.

vi)   There should be effective operators.

vii)   The equipment should be multi-purpose so as to accomplish various functions simultaneously.

viii)   There should be plenty of spare parts to enable the equipment to be promptly repaired when need arises.

CHAPTER TEN

MANAGEMENT CAREERS

Introduction

Management careers tend to evolve through a series of stages. Individual career do not necessarily follow a similar pattern. It is therefore hard to understand where managers are in their careers and what shape the future may be

.

Definition of career

A career is sequence of work experiences which accumulates over a manager's working life more or less successfully.

Career Stages

I. Exploration Stage

The first stage is one of exploration which occurs at the beginning of a career and it is characterized by self analysis and the exploration of the different types of available jobs. In this stage people hold part time jobs while in school or college which enable them to understand the types of career they would want to pursue. This stage occurs between 18 to 25 years.

ii. Establishment Stage

The second stage occurs when the career path is established. Jobs may now establish a pattern where the experiences of the exploration stage are put into practice and each job is sought as a progression on the previous one. Promotion is sought in the same company or in different companies and a career pattern begins to develop. This stage occurs between 25 to 35 years.

iii. Maintenance and Growth Stage

The third stage in career evolution is the maintenance and growth stage. The established career is maintained and nurtured. The manager's career may stabilize at this stage, grow or even stagnate. It is particularly at this point that careers may reach a plateau where there is little further development. This stage occurs from 25 years and has no limit.

iv. Plateau Stage

This is a stage in which manager's career has little development. It may arise due to low level of performance, bad luck, and poor assessment by superiors or due to stiff competition for fewer top management positions.

This stage occurs between 35 and 55 years.

v. Decline Stage

Decline stage usually occurs near the retirement when managers may not be able to maintain prior performance levels because of loss of interest or difficulty in keeping their job skills up to date.

This stage may occur from 55 years onwards.

Career and life cycle

Manager careers follow a progressive sequence. Most manager's career depict the cycle (see the diagram below).

High

Decline stage

Performance

and pay   Maintenance   Plateau stage

     stage

        Exploration stage   Establishment

Low   stage

  18   25   35   45   55

65

               Age

Careers Mobility:-

Managers' careers are mobile although some managers have immobile careers.

Factors that influence career mobility:

i.   Management schools are unfairly distributed. Managers that want to improve their managerial skills move closer to the schools.

ii.   Global market characteristics are becoming identical and, therefore, managers are motivated to move their careers to different zones.

iii.   The world is becoming insecure. Most managers move their careers to secure environment.

iv.   Some managers will move their careers to the environment which is more suitable to their health.

v.   Social pressures will influence managers to move their careers to the environment in which they can meet social contacts.

vi.   Some managers move their careers to the organizations that improve their empirical knowledge.

vii.   Family unity is very vital. Managers whose families have been separated will always move their careers to be together with their families.

viii.   The rate of technology is rapidly changing. Managers that are not able to cope with the rapid rate, move their careers to other slow organizations..

Career Development

Management careers have become very competitive. Managers are therefore encouraged to develop their careers to remain competitive.

Career development approaches are:-

i.   Registration in a management school and pursuing management training.

ii.   Participation in management development courses such as seminars, conferences etc.

iii.   Read management journals from different schools of management so as to improve on empirical knowledge.

iv.   Associating, mostly, with other managers.

v.   Read management topics in print media.

vi.   Listening to the contributions of management experts on electronic media.

vii.   Read management text books.

viii.   Watch films on management topics.

Women and management careers:-

Women appear to have lagged behind men in management careers not only in Kenya but also in most countries.

Factors that cause women to lag behind men are:-

i.   Cultural

        Most families favour boys more than girls, especially in the education development, which enable

        boys to acquire qualifications that make them to be admitted in management institutions.

ii.   Biological

        Women become mothers; they tend to become ineffective during the motherhood situations.

iii.   Women are very conscious of their ethical standards. Most women are reluctant to go to social places unaccompanied, the trend which makes them not to network.

iv.   Lifestyles of women managers is very arduous; most of them seek retirement very early in their careers.

v.   Most husbands do not support their wives in management career development. Infact, some husbands discourage their wives from pursuing management careers.

vi.   Most top women managers do not support upcoming junior women managers in career development.

vii.   Because most top management positions are held by men, women are discouraged from applying for these positions because they feel that they cannot be democratically assessed.

viii.   Management jobs keep top managers away from their homes for long periods. This trend is not ideal, especially for married women managers , therefore they seek early retirement.

Career Planning

Career planning is the systematic process by which one selects career goals and path goals. From the organization's view point, it means helping the employees to plan their career in terms of their capacities within the context of organization's needs. It involves designing an organizational system of career movement and growth opportunities for employees from establishment stage to decline and retirement stages for individuals who can fill planned future positions. It is a managerial technique for mapping out the entire career of young employees. It requires discovery, development, planned employment and re-employment of talents.

The main characteristics of career planning:-

i)   Career planning is a process of developing human resources rather than an event.

ii)   It is not an end in itself but a means of managing people to obtain optimum results.

iii)   Career planning is an individual responsibility but also is the responsibility of an organization to provide guidance and counseling to its employees in planning their careers and developing and utilizing their knowledge and skills.

iv)   Goals of employees should be integrated with organizational goals.

v)   The basic aim of career planning is integration of individual and organizational needs.

Objectives of career planning are:-

i)   To attract and retain the right type of persons in the organization.

ii)   To map out careers of employees suitable to their willingness to be trained and develop for higher positions.

iii)   To ensure better use of human resources through more satisfied and productive employees.

iv)   To have a more stable workforce by reducing absenteeism and labour turnover.

v)   To increasingly utilize the managerial talent available at all levels within the organization.

vi)   To improve employees morale and motivation by matching skills to job requirements and by providing opportunities for promotions.

vii)   To ensure that promising employees get experiences that will equip them to reach responsibility for which they are able.

viii)   To provide guidance and encourage employees to fulfill their potentials.

ix)   To achieve higher productivity and organizational development.

Career planning process

The process involves the following steps:-

i)   Identify needs and aspirations

First of all, an objective analysis of the hopes and aspirations of different categories of employees is done. It is necessary to identify and communicate the career goals, aspirations and career anchors of every employee because most individuals may not have a clear idea about these. Proper personnel inventory that reveals the age, qualifications, experience and aptitude of present employees should be kept. An appraisal of existing employees is enforced to identify the most suitable employee.

ii)   Analyzing career opportunities

The organization set up plans and careers system of the employees are analyzed to identify opportunities available within it. Career path can be determined for each employee.

iii)   Identifying match and mismatch

A mechanism for identifying suitability between individual current aspirations and organizational career system is developed to identify and compare specific areas of match and mismatch for different career opportunities. Such matching helps to develop realistic career goals for both long term and short term. For this purpose specific jobs are related to different career opportunities.

iv)   Formulating and implementing strategies

Alternative strategies and action plans for dealing with mismatch are formulated and implemented.

v)   Reviewing career plans

A periodic review of career plans is necessary to know whether the plans are contributing to effective utilization of human resources by matching employee objectives to jobs' needs.

Factors that contribute to career effectiveness:-

i)   Expansion career: Career planning is feasible in growing organizations.

ii)   Career goals: An organization must have clear corporate goals for the next decade.

iii)   Motivated and hardworking staff: An organization with motivated and hardworking staff can create an environment that is ideal for development.

iv)   Proper selection: selection of right jobs is essential for career planning.

v)   Proper age balance: Unbalanced age structure causes promotion blocks which hampers career planning.

vi)   Fair promotion policy: There should be an equitable policy for promoting employees.

vii)   Top management support: Strong and unflinching co-operation of top management is most important for effective career planning.

viii)   Management of career stress: Stress at work is harmful to an individual's career as well as to the organization. Management is encouraged to conduct 'stress management' courses for its staff.

Advantages of career planning:-

i)   It helps an employee to know the career opportunities available in an organization.

ii)   Career knowledge enables the employees to select the career most suitable to their potential and aptitude.

iii)   It can attract competent employees.

iv)   It helps to retain hardworking and talented employees.

v)   It is a participative process and under it job assignments are based on merit alone. This helps to improve employee morale and productivity.

vi)   Anticipates the future vacancies that may arise due to retirement, resignation, death at managerial level.

vii)   Facilitates expansion and growth of the enterprise.

viii)   It helps to improve employee morale and productivity.

CHAPTER ELEVEN

MANAGEMENT ENHANCEMENT SKILLS

Chapter 11/1 STRESS MANAGEMENT

Introduction

Every person is stressed although most people will never know that they are stressed until some illness manifest itself.

Stress is therefore a consequence of or a general response to an action or situation that places special physical or psychological demands or both, on a person.

It involves the interaction of a person and that person's environment.

Definition

Stress is an internal response to external stimuli (forces) affecting an individual, organization or system.

Stressors

These are physical or psychological demands from environment that cause stress. Demands could also be cultural, financial, social or political.

Fight or flight response

This refers to biochemical and bodily changes that occur as a naturally response to an environmental stressor. That is, in response to a perceived stressor, the human nervous system prepares the body to overcome stress effects.

General Adaptation Syndrome (GAS)

This syndrome constitutes the three phases of the defense reaction a person establishes when stressed.

Elaboration of GAS:-

I.   General: Defense reaction is called general because stressors have effects on several areas of the body.

ii.   Adaptation: This refers to a stimulation of defense designed to help body to adjust or deal with stressors.

iii.   Syndrome: Indicates that individual pieces of the reaction occur more and less together.

GAS three distinct phases or stages:-

i.   Alarm stage

This is the initial mobilization by which the body meets the challenge posed by stressors, e.g. when stressor is recognized, the brain sends forth a biochemical message to all body's system or parts. An individual thus can observe, respiration increases, blood pressure rises, pupils (eyes) dilate, muscles tense up etc

ii.   Resistance stage

If sensors continue, the GAS proceeds to the resistance stage.

Signs of being in resistance stage include fatigue, anxiety and tension. These signs are/or exhibited because the individual is fighting stressors.

While resistance to a particular stressor may be high during this stage, resistance to others (stressors) may be low.

A person has only finite sources of energy, concentration and ability to resist stressors.

iii.   Exhaustion

Is GAS final stage:-

i.   This is stage whereby prolonged and continual exposure to the same stressor eventually uses up or exhausts the adaptive energy available, i.e. the system of fighting the stressors is exhausted.

ii.   Mind and body have limits. This stressor tears and wears the psychological mechanism.

iii.   The more the person is alarmed, exhausted by work and non work interaction, the more susceptible he becomes fatigued, sick , ageing and also witnesses other negative stress consequences.

Sources of work stress:

Sources intrinsic to the job:-

i.   Too much or too little work

ii.   Poor physical working conditions

iii.   Time pressure and deadlines

iv.   Social isolation at work

v.   Interpersonal conflict

vi.   Excessive travel

vii.   Performing monotonous work

viii.   Long hours of work

Sources from career development:-

i.   Over promotion

ii.   Under promotion

iii.   Lack of job security

iv.   Thwarted or shattered ambitions

v.   Perception that one's situation is problematic

vi.   Placed on a job that one is not qualified

Sources from relations within the organization:-

i.   Poor relations with bosses

ii.   Poor relations with colleagues

iii.   Lack of communication

iv.   Lack of confidence of the juniors

v.   Partiality

Being in the organization:-

i.   Lack of effective consultation

ii.   Restriction on behavior

iii.   Office politics

iv.   Frequent shift work

v.   No sense of belonging

Symptoms of stress:-

i.   Absenteeism

ii.   Tardiness i.e absence from the working desk while a worker is within the organization.

iii.   Lack of motivation to work

iv.   Absence of suggestions to employer

v.   Erratic temper

vi.   Withdrawal from others

vii.   Failure to achieve work targets

viii.   Development of high blood pressure

ix.   Development of duodenal ulcer which occurs due to intensive thinking

x.   Suffering from some of skin diseases

xi.   Headaches especially on one side of the head which leads to impairness of vision

xii.   Some forms of diarrhea

xiii.   Insomnia (lack of sleep)

xiv.   Lack of appetite

xv.   Irritability

xvi.   Escapist drinking

xvii.   Nervousness

xviii. Migraine- accompanied by vomiting and weakness on one side of the head

xix.   Depression- which sometimes leads to suicide

xx.   Sweating

xxi.   Hot and cold flashes

xxii.   Mouth dryness

xxiii. Accident proneness

xxiv. Drug problem or misuse

xxv.   Excessive smoking

xxvi. Under or overeating

xxvii. Lowliness

xxviii. Low self esteem

xxix. Job dissatisfaction

xxx.   Reduced organization commitment or loyalty

Personal methods of coping with stress:-

i.   Assess the stress in relation to job design, organization goals and expectation of an individual.

ii.   Organize your time at work, only do things that are very important and things that are urgent.

iii.   Learn to do one thing at a time.

iv.   Be realistic by knowing your concentration span and energy curve.

v.   Concentrate on one task at a time.

vi.   Try to maintain a balanced system.

vii.   Develop clear and defined working goals.

viii.   Participate in sports.

ix.   Walk during lunch time.

x.   Vent: yell, cry.

Indicators of stressors in the work place:-

i.   Managers in organizations might become aware of stress problems by being capable or able to recognize employees' symptoms of excessive stress.

ii.   Excessive stress include changes in personality, work habits or behaviour pattern e.g. a jovial employee could become dull or different.

iii.   Stressed employees withdraw from other colleagues.

iv.   The rate of absenteeism among stressed employees increases.

v.   The rate of conflict increases among stressed people.

vi.   There is high percentage of gossip among stressed employees.

vii.   Employees health deteriorates.

Approaches taken by management to help stressed employees cope with stress

i.   Help stressed employees cope with stress.

ii.   Change physical environment.

iii.   Redesign the job if stressors are role conflict.

iv.   Change organization structural design.

v.   Conduct career counseling sessions for stressed employees.

vi.   Conduct physical fitness programs for stressed employees.

vii.   Conduct job-burn out seminars and workshops for stressed employees.

viii.   Conduct role redefinition workshops for stressed employees.

Effects of consequences of stress:-

Positive effects:

1   Self motivation

2   Stimulation to work harder

3   Increased inspiration to live better life

    Negative effects

1   Total negative thinking

2   Self hatred

3   Feeling hopeless

Job burnout

Definition

It is adverse effect of working conditions where stressors seem unavoidable and sources of satisfaction or relief seem unavailable.

Job burnout exists in the following situation:-

i.   The job contains a larger number of stressors and means to manage are not available.

ii.   The job characteristics make the job incumbent seek an attainable goals or an achievable goals.

iii.   The present stressors remain for a long time or a period of time.

iv.   The job incumbent is very idealistic and a high achiever when resistance resources are really overworked.

The path to job burnout:-

Working conditions e.g.

i.   Constant pressure

ii.   Insecurity

iii.   Competition pressures

iv.   Overspecialization

v.   Conflicts

vi.   Economic problems

vii.   Health problems

viii.   Alienation

ix.   Uncertainty

x.   Isolation

Characterized by:-

i.   Unfulfilled expectations

ii.   Lack of challenge

iii.   Lack of meaning

iv.   Lack of control

v.   Limited mobility

vi.   Overwork

vii.   Poor decisions

viii.   Lack of focus

Leads to:-

i.   Stress

ii.   Fatigue

iii.   Frustrations

iv.   Helplessness

v.   Guilt

vi.   Low self esteem

vii.   Job burnout

Note: Poor working conditions or say, so many stress and resolutions to solve them culminate into job burnout.

LEARN TO RELAX

Techniques:-

1.   Relaxation response

This is an anti stress response in which muscle tension, heart rate and blood pressure decrease and breathing slows.

Relaxation response process:-

i.   Sit quietly in a comfortable position.

ii.   Close your eyes.

iii.   Deeply relax all muscles, beginning at your feet and progressing up to your face. Keep all muscles relaxed.

iv.   Breathe through your nose. Become aware of your breathing. As you breathe out, say the word 'one' silently to yourself. For example breathe in...........out, 'one' in ....out, 'two' and so on. Breathe easily and naturally you might also say the words 'calm' or 'let go' as you exhale

v.   Continue for 10 to 20 minutes. As you feel yourself relax, try to visualize your favorite place- a beach, lake or a mountain stream. Try picture in detail and recall feelings of peace and contentment while being there. You may open your eyes to check the time, but do not use an alarm. When you finish, sit quietly for several minutes, at first with your eyes closed and later with your eyes open. Do not stand up for a few minutes.

vi.   Don't worry about whether you are successful in achieving a deep level of relaxation. Maintain a passive attitude and permit relation to occur at its own pace. When distracting thoughts occurs try to ignore them by not dwelling on them and return to repeating 'one'. With practice, the response should come with little effort.

Practice the technique once or twice daily, but not within two hours of any meal because the digestive process seems to interfere with elicitation of the relaxation response.

Transcendental Meditation (TM)

This is a popular form of meditation that involves sitting comfortable with eyes closed and engaging in the repetition of a special sound for 20 minutes twice a day. Studies show that TM is related to reduced heart rate, lowered oxygen consumption, and decreased blood pressure. Medical evidence indicates that practicing TM may help unclog arteries, especially the people with high blood pressure.

Meditation has also been shown to alleviate lower back pain, headaches and arthritis, decrease absenteeism, tardiness and labour turn over, increase brain wave activity and also improve concentration.

Chapter 11/2: TIME MANAGEMENT

Introduction

'Time is like a river; you cannot touch same water twice, because the flow that has passed will never pass again'.

Management goals and employees goals become incompatible because of ever arising environment forces which pull the said goals in opposite directions. To bridge the gap between management goals and employees goals compel the management to spend a lot of time which, if not planned, make management fail to achieve the set objectives. Management is therefore, forced to effectively manage time.

Definition

Time management is a systematic step approach to using time effectively.

Time wasters:-

i.   Lack of focus on time i.e poor direction, lack of understanding.

ii.   Managers' failure to delegate.

iii.   Interruptions by visitors, relatives, staff.

iv.   Holding unplanned meetings.

v.   Gossip (note, gossip involves more than one person).

vi.   Stress (stressed staff will not concentrate on their work).

vii.   Tiredness.

viii.   Tardiness (frequent movement to other offices without any valid reason).

Skills for managing time:-

i.   Identify tasks and priorities

Plan your workload by making lists of work to be done in sequence order; these include master list and specific daily list.

ii.   The master list

This is a single, continuous list maintained in a spiral bound or small loose leaf notebook, of everything you have to do.

iii.   The daily list

The list includes tasks that have to be performed the following day. The daily list should be developed at the end of each day.

Time program design:-

Steps:

i.   Divide your work daily into 'public activities' and 'private activities'.

ii.   Select the most demanding activities and schedule them into your morning or afternoon prime time block. For most people, these will be private activities like writing or planning.

iii.   Schedule less demanding tasks in blocks during 'lower' time.

iv.   Group meetings, appointments and phone calls into a 'public' block either morning or afternoon.

v.   Spend half an hour reading during a 5.00 pm pause.

vi.   Alternatively group activities into weekly pattern. For example;

·   Reserve Mondays and Tuesdays for writing and planning.

·   Use the rest of the week for public contacts.

·   Consolidate regular staff meetings into one day instead of distributing them throughout the week.

Techniques of mastering the time wasters:-

i.   Limit your control to specific phases of time i.e. prime time, occasional private work periods

ii.   Schedule appointments and deal with rest of the day more flexibly.

iii.   Ask your staff not to disturb you during designated interruption free periods. It is advisable to put this request in writing.

iv.   Set a specific day to attend to private matters, for example, visitors, family members have to pass through the secretary unless the matter demands prompts attention.

v.   Ask your secretary to shelter you from interruptions with all diplomacy and muscle she can master.

vi.   Supply your secretary with a list of callers to whom you will always speak (boss is an important client) and those whose calls you will take only at specified times under certain circumstances.

vii.   If you do not have a secretary, arrange an exchange with a colleague, taking each other's calls during designated periods.

viii.   Install a telephone answering machine.

ix.   Consolidate call backs: return all calls at one time beginning with priority calls.

x.   Time your return calls: call back when people are less inclined to chat i.e right before lunch or near the end of the day.

Methods of controlling numerous and lengthy visits:-

A certain amount of inter office visiting fosters a harmonious working environment. However, when brief visits escalates into numerous and lengthy sessions, one can enforce the following approaches:

i.   When possible, angle your secretary's desk so she can effectively intercept all visitors. Ask her to politely schedule an appointment with the visitor or suggest that the person come by at another specified day.

ii.   If you do not have a secretary, keep your door closed during private work sessions

iii.   Post a sign on your door or desk saying ' working privately', for example, between 9.00 and 10.30 am, 'Please come later'.

iv.   If you work in an open office, angle your desk so that you avoid catching the eye of passersby.

v.   Work at home, one or two mornings a week.

vi.   Decamp to library or empty conference room.

vii.   Take colleagues to a hotel for long range planning or brainstorming sessions.

viii.   Consolidate visitors by scheduling appointments and meetings into specific blocks of time. The most practical method is to establish specific 'open house' hours every day or several times a week, and encourage people to time their visits accordingly.

ix.   Set limits: it is advisable to plan the time each topic should take; open ended talks waste much time.

x.   Confer in colleague's offices. When colleagues ask to confer with you, try to meet in their offices rather than yours. It is much easier to excuse yourself than to ease someone out.

xi.   When an interruption is inevitable whether phone call or visit, it is helpful to stop writing in mid sentence. It is also advisable to jot down a couple of key words to help pick up the process later.

Management of staff time:-

In military circles, there is a saying that, 'there is no good or bad soldier but good and bad officers'.

The above saying confirms the statement that behaviour of juniors reflect the behavior of the top.

Most organizations that experience poor management of time can be traced from mismanagement of time by top managers.

Staff waste their time in almost the same ways as managers.

Methods of managing staff time:-

1. Clock in the office

Every office should have a wall clock to enable staff manage their time. One cannot effectively manage time if one is not guided by a clock or a watch.

2.   Time recording method

i. Autographic machine

The machine has a clock mechanism which controls paper tape. When recording his time, an employee presses the handle at the side of the machine which automatically records the time on the tape and at the same time releases a shutter over the tape, so that one can sign one's name opposite printed time. On releasing the handle, the shutter closes the aperture until next entry.

The machine is ideal for employees that are required to report on time because of their work demand.

The machine is automatic, fraud proof and also provides printed times, reveals lateness and overtime.

        ii. Time card recorder (time clocks)

The time card recorder is based on an individual time records for each worker- the time card. The recording clock is flanked on each side by card racks 'in' being on one side of it and 'out' on the other.

This card has some of the following benefits:

·   Lateness and overtime are usually printed in red (ordinary time in black or blue).

· An individual time record is created and attendance for the whole week are on the card.

· A visual check on the absentees can be made every morning.

3. Watchman's detector

There are various types of time recorders for recording times at which watchmen visit a number of fixed points on their patrol.

The most usual type consists of portable recorders slung around the watchmen's neck and on which he clocks with special keys located at various patrol points.

This method is ideal because it makes the watchman alert, mobile and compelled to reach strategic sites especially at night.

iv.   Reduce employees' paper work, for example, by using form letters.

v.   Train subordinates to listen by questions and answer techniques

vi.   Set time standards for jobs

vii.   Advise juniors to do one thing at a time

viii.   Advise employees not to receive visitors during working time.

ix.   Advise employees to consult experienced colleagues when they encounter any problem.

Chapter 11/3: Delegation

Introduction

In working areas, managers perform various functions and also make different decisions such as administrative, operational and strategic.

Definition

Delegation is a process of passing some of the manager's functions to juniors.

Principles of delegation:-

i.   Delegation should be vertical i.e down the departmental line organization.

ii.   Delegation should be done one step at a time i.e one superior delegates to one subordinate, his subordinate. If relevant, the subordinate delegates one step down to his immediate subordinate and so on.

iii.   Delegation must be specific i.e. the supervisor must ensure that delegate knows clearly the extent of his tasks, responsibilities etc preferably in writing.

iv.   The delegator must ensure that he has clearly defined the results expected. Ambiguous instructions must be avoided.

v.   Follow unity of command and chain of command. Ideally authority should be delegated so that each individual reports to only one superior.

vi.   A delegator must give moral as well as material support to subordinates with delegated authority. Advise and encouragement should be given to reward subordinates for successful assumption of authority.

vii.   Suitable financial and non financial incentives should be provided to reward subordinates for successful assumption of authority.

viii.   Delegation should go down the line as far as possible to ensure effective utilization of human and material resources.

ix.   The superior should be held responsible for communicating to the company and its relevant members the delegated tasks and authority.

Indicators of non delegation:-

i.   Manager's desk usually has a pile of files or records.

ii. Managers carry home unfinished work after duty to complete it at home.

iii. Managers that don't delegate complete their woks on weekends.

iv. Non delegators work extra hours after the end of the day.

v. Bad relations develop between non delegators with their hard working employees who get stressed when not given any work.

vi. Non delegators suffer from stress related problems such as high blood pressure, insomnia, duodenal ulcers etc due to overworking themselves.

Factors that discourage delegation:-

i.   Managers lack of confidence in subordinates.

ii.   Some managers fail to delegate so as to portray themselves as very hardworking.

iii.   Some managers who have been involved in fraud will not delegate to cover the fraud.

iv.   Fear of some managers being challenged by their subordinates will discourage them from delegating to their subordinates.

v.   Some managers will avoid delegating to their subordinates so as to avoid their positions being taken from by their juniors.

vi.   Managers decline to delegate to avoid expanding span of control.

Factors that encourage delegation:-

i.   It becomes necessary to delegate to a subordinate who is being prepared for promotion.

ii.   A manager will be forced to delegate if he has to meet deadline.

iii.   When the work volume becomes too much, a manager is compelled to delegate

iv.   The necessity to develop a successor will encourage the manager to delegate to the subordinate being prepared for the position.

v.   Weak managers delegate to their subordinates so as to conceal their weaknesses.

vi.   Manager will delegate to enable a subordinate to acquire experience.

Advantages of delegation:-

i.   Few managers have the time to handle their own jobs and jobs of their subordinates.

ii.   Subordinates take pride in results that are directly attributable to their own judgment.

iii.   Delegation helps to develop the talents and abilities of subordinates.

iv.   Delegation enriches the subordinates' job. The approach motivates the subordinates.

v.   Delegation improves the relations between the manager and his subordinates.

vi.   Organizations that encourage delegation policy have low rate of staff conflict.

vii.   Because of low rate of staff conflict in organizations that encourage delegation, the organization acquires a positive corporate image.

viii.   The organizations which have acquired a positive corporate image caused by delegation develop high demand for their services or products.

Disadvantages of delegation:-

i.   Trade secrets are likely to be leaked by delegates.

ii.   Some delegates are not able to achieve targets on time.

iii.   Delegation increases manager's span of control which overworks him.

iv.   Weak managers hide behind delegates.

v.   The quality of work produced by delegates sometimes is of low quality.

vi.   Some subordinates have the impression that the manager delegates because he is not able to perform.

vii.   Some subordinates deliberately give wrong results to undermine their superior.

viii.   Some inexperienced delegates spoil equipment and machines used while performing delegated work.

Chapter 11/4: PLANNING

Introduction

Planning is the most important managerial function. Everyone has a plan either formally or informally. Every person is involved in planning various activities, for example, at work, at school, home and in other places.

The primary purpose for planning is to provide guidelines necessary for decision making and the resulting action throughout the organization. Plans give purpose to our lives and formalized plans enable managers to mobilize their intentions to accomplish organizational purposes.

Planning deals with the future uncertainty and it is necessary for a manager to be flexible. Through planning, managers are able to have clue of the future.

Good planning is essential for good performance of other managerial functions. Planning involves selecting from among alternative future causes of actions for entire organization and for every department and sections within.

Definition

Planning is the design of the desired future and effective ways of bringing it about.

Types of Plan:-

I. Objectives

An objectives is a specific commitment within a given time frame.

Objectives are ends towards which activities in an organization are aimed, for example, to earn a profit or provide a certain service. Objectives determine how the various scarce resources in an organization will be used.

ii. Mission

A mission is the purpose and it provides an organization with direction. A mission statement offers guidelines to management and it should be followed during the development of strategies. It is general and visionary. It identifies the basic function or task of an organization.

iii. Strategy

A strategy is a calculated means by which an enterprise will deploy its resources to accomplish its purpose and objectives under the most advantageous circumstances and conditions forecast or projected.

Strategies follow on from the determination of long term goals and objectives

iv.   A policy

A policy is a general statement 'or understandings' which provides guidelines for management decision making.

Company policies might be for example:

·   To offer 5 years guarantees on products sold and give money back to customers with valid complaints.

·   To promote managers from within the organization whenever possible instead of recruiting manages to senior positions from outside.

·   To encourage all recruits to certain jobs within the organization to work towards obtaining an appropriate professional qualifications.

·   To be price-competitive in the market.

v. Procedures

Procedures are chronological sequence of required actions for performing a certain task. Procedures exist at all levels of management. Procedures become more numerous at the lower organization's hierarchy.

vi. Rules

A rule is a specific definite course of action that must be taken into a given situation.

Examples of rules:-

· Employees in department X are allowed 10 minutes exactly at the end of their shift for clearing up and cleaning their work benches.

· Employees with access to a telephone must not use the telephone for personal calls.

vii. A budget

A budget is a formal statement of expected results set out in numerical terms, and summarized in money values. It is a plan for carrying out certain activities within a given period of time in order to achieve certain targets. The budget indicates how many resources will be allocated to each department or activity in order to carry out the planned activities.

The budget is usually prepared on a companywide or organization wide basis, so that all the activities of the organization are coordinated within a single plan.

Principles of good planning:-

i. Planning exercise should be as systematic as possible i.e. planning steps should flow in an orderly manner.

ii. Planning should be based on adequate information.

iii. Planning should be comprehensive i.e. must be complete taking into account all the stages of actions.

iv. Planning should be realistic.

v. Planning should be based on accurate information i.e. no guess work.

vi. The plan implementation should be practised.

vii. Planning exercise should be simple, i.e. every person should understand it.

viii.   Planning process should be focused.

The steps in planning

The steps in a planning decision are:-

i.   Recognize an opportunity to be exploited or a problem to be dealt with.

ii.   Establish goals or objectives as the end result of exploiting the opportunity or solving the problem.

iii.   Obtain forecasts of relevant information (e.g about products, markets, competition, prices, wage rates technology etc)

iv.   Consider alternative realistic courses of action for the achievement of the objectives.

v.   Compare the alternative courses of action, and selecting the best course.

vi.   Formulate detailed plans for carrying out the chosen course of action.

vii.   Implement action.

viii.   Carry out feedback exercise to ensure the plan has achieved the goal.

Barriers to good planning:-

i.   Lack of knowledge about the purpose and goals of the organization. Unless a manager knows what the organization's goals are, and how other departments and sections are trying to work towards those goals, his own efforts might conflict with the efforts of someone else.

ii.   A reluctance to be commitment to one set of targets.

iii.   Fear of blame or criticism for failing to achieve planned targets.

iv.   Manager's lack of confidence in himself to perform his job efficiently and effectively.

v.   Manager's negative attitude towards planning i.e., some managers believe that the future cannot be predicted accurately.

vi.   Planning is based on forecasts which are never 100% accurate i.e. accurate goal is not possible since the future cannot be predicted with complete accuracy.

vii.   Planning is a time consumer, so most managers avoid effective planning.

viii.   Planning is expensive so most managers are discouraged to have a thorough planning.

ix. Planning premises should be established which are agreed and used by managers

Methods of overcoming barriers to effective planning:-

i.   All levels of staff should be involved (to a greater or less degree) in planning process.

ii.   Planners must be provided with the information they need i.e. should have access to sources of future information when the need arises so as to plan properly.

iii.   Managers should be taught the virtues of planning and the techniques of good planning.

iv.   Planning must be definite, time specific and focused.

v.   Plans should be flexible to allow for change so as to adapt to the changing environment.

vi.   Long range planning must be integrated properly with short range planning.

vii.   Plans should be reviewed regularly in order to identify shortcomings and to allow for adjustments when necessary.

viii.   A system of rewards for successful achievement of plans will motivate those who have had successful plans and also encourage those who have succeeded to work harder.

Advantages of good planning:-

i.   It gives a clear sense of direction and purpose.

ii.   It maximizes the chances for achieving goals.

iii.   Helps in making the work orderly and focused especially in an organizational set up.

iv.   It prioritizes goals and objectives such that the most valuable ones are given the highest priority.

v.   It provides a challenge and clear expectations to managers.

vi.   Provides a basis for measuring organizational and individual performance.

vii.   Good planning enables the organization to maximize production.

viii.   Good planning enable managers and staff to work harmoniously.

CHAPTER TWELVE

EMERGING TRENDS IN MANAGEMENT

Chapter 12/1: LEARNING ORGANIZATIONS

Introduction

Learning organization has been a focus of attention in the organization literature. Interest in organizational development (OD) intervention has been spurred by the constantly changing work and business environments which have been prompted by technological advances, increased level of competition and globalization of industries.

Definitions

i.   Learning organization is a group of people working together to collectively enhance their capacities so as to create results that they truly care about .(Peter Senge, 2004)

ii.   Learning organization is the organization which facilitates the learning of all its members and continuously transforms it. (Pedler, Boyle & Burgoyne)

Levels Of Learning Organization:-

Level one: This level focuses on the development, production and marketing of products and services.

Level two: This level is involved in designing and development of systems and processes.

Level three: This level undertakes and coordinates the tasks of level one and two.

Characteristics of learning organization:-

i.   Actively try to infuse their organizations with new ideas and information.

ii.   Continually transfer knowledge throughout the organization.

iii.   Strive to reduce structural processes and interpersonal barriers to the sharing of information, ideas and knowledge among organization members.

iv.   Learning organizations are result oriented.

v.   Foster environment in which employees are encouraged to use new behaviour and operational processes to achieve corporate goals.

vi.   Proactively create, acquire, transfer knowledge and its behaviour on the basis of new knowledge and insights.

vii.   Change behaviour on the basis of new knowledge and insights.

Principles of learning organization:-

i.   Learning should occur at the system level than at the operation (individual) level.

ii.   Learning should transform the organization in a direction that is increasingly satisfying to its shareholders.

iii.   Learning should arise from processes surrounding the sharing of insights, knowledge and mental models.

iv.   Learning should be embedded in the culture, organizational systems, procedures and processes.

v.   Learning should be encouraged and rewarded.

vi.   Learning should intentionally use learning at the individual group and system level.

vii.   Learning should be keenly perceived at the system level.

Strategies ideal for promoting learning organizations:-

i.   Create continuous learning opportunities.

ii.   Promote inquiry and dialogue.

iii.   Encourage collaboration and team learning.

iv.   Establish systems to capture and share learning.

v.   Empower people towards a collective vision.

vi.   Connect the organization to its environment.

vii.   Reshape organization's culture to support continual learning.

viii. Redesigning the organization's structure to reduce boundaries between people and to increase interdependence.

ix.   Make explicit commitment to change innovation and continuous learning.

Importance of a successful learning organization:-

i.   Enables the organizations to achieve their mission.

ii.   Learning organizations improve employees' job attitudes.

iii.   They improve relations between the management and employees.

iv.   They develop personal mastery of work by employees.

v.   Shared vision of the organization development among management and employees enhance the degree of their cohesiveness.

vi.   Enables the management to easily restructure the organization.

vii.   Enables the management to improve human resource practices.

viii. Enables management to improve the enforcement of management and leadership styles.

Chapter 12/2: BUSINESS PROCESSING RE ENGINEERING

Introduction

Managers operations have continued to be difficult because of ever arising environmental forces caused by rapid rate of technology development.

Due to this trend, Hammer and Champy in 1993 conducted a seminar to formulate techniques that should be enforced by managers to increase and maintain efficient and effective business operations.

Definition

Re-engineering is the fundamental re-thinking and radical redesign of business processes to achieve dramatic improvements in critical contemporary measures of performances, such as cost, quality, services and speed.

Re- engineering techniques:-

i.   Jobs or tasks which are related should be combined to save time.

ii.   Workers should be empowered by involving them in decision making.

iii.   Work should be performed where it makes most sense. For example the business owner or his representative should control the cash box.

iv.   Workers should be left to work on their own after the induction course. This approach builds their confidence and maximizes their production.

v.   A single person should be appointed to fill the position of a customer service representative.

vi.   Operations should be centralized in the form of a shared data base.

vii.   During the operations process, two or more operations should be combined. For example past examination question papers be revised during the lecture session.

viii.   Workers should be trained to improve their performance.

Characteristics of a re- engineered organization:-

i.   Work structures move away from functional departments towards process teams.

ii.   Employees are empowered to act in ways that were previously controlled by rules or regulations.

iii.   Empowerment implies a willingness and ability to accept greater responsibility.

iv.   The focus of performance and payments shifts from activities to results.

v.   Advancement within the organization is more likely to be based on the ability to perform more advanced   future jobs than the current one.

Advantages of re- engineering staff:-

i.   Re engineered staff tend to be more effective than non re-engineered ones.

ii.   Re- engineered staff experience less degree of fatigue than non re-engineered ones.

iii.   Organizations with re-engineered employees can easily down size staff without causing conflict. This is because remaining staff will cope with increased workload.

iv.   Employees in a re-engineered organization tend to be more cohesive because all are well informed.

v.   Relation between management and re-engineered staff tends to be cordial.

vi.   Positive results derived from re-engineered organizations enable the organization to acquire a positive image.

vii.   Re engineered organizations attract more customers because they expect to get better services.

viii.   Re-engineered organizations have a low rate of labour turnover.

Disadvantages of re-engineered staff:-

i.   Re-engineered employees cause conflict between themselves and management when management decline to promote them.

ii.   Re- engineered employees are very mobile i.e they often resign to take up higher positions in other organizations.

iii.   When re-engineered employees   fail to be rewarded by the employer, They get frustrated hence leak trade secrets.

iv.   Bickering by re-engineered employees due to the failure to reward them, discourage those who would like to join the organization.

v.   The negative cumulative effects caused by unsatisfied re-engineered employees negatively affect the organization corporate image which lead to the reduction of output.

Chapter 12/3: KNOWLEDGE MANAGEMENT

Introduction

Knowledge management is one of the emerging trends in the fast changing environmental developments.

Typically, knowledge management programmes involve using technology to establish repository data bases and retrieval systems. These are ways of using computers to sort through and identify the areas of expertise represented in the company- that is, in intellectual capital.

Knowledge management relies on human skills for success. Computers merely organize what those skills are and where in the company they may be found.

Knowledge management is also concerned with the management of work practices with the goal of improving the sharing of the information (knowledge) in organizations.

Knowledge management also involves holistic view of information, planning, controlling, coordinating information and also consolidating formal and informal information.

Definition

i.   Knowledge management is the discipline that promotes an integrated approach to identifying, managing and sharing all of the organizations information assets.

ii.   Knowledge management is the process of capturing and making use of a firm's collective expertise anywhere in the business on paper, in documents, in data bases (called explicit knowledge), or in people's heads (called tacit knowledge)

Types of knowledge management:-.

i.   Explicit knowledge

This is knowledge codified and digitized in books, documents, reports, memos, training courses.

Explicit knowledge can be retrieved and transmitted more easily than tacit knowledge.

Explicit knowledge is easier to identify because it is a physical entity that can be measured and distributed.

Knowledge management is stored as a written procedure or as a process in a computer.

It is revisable for decision making purposes.

ii.   Tacit knowledge

This is knowledge embedded in the human mind through experience and jobs.

It includes intuitions, values and beliefs that stem from years of experience.

It is the knowledge used to create explicit knowledge and is best communicated personally through dialogue and scenarios, with use of metaphors.

Note: socially relayed knowledge becomes part of the real life experience of the knowledge.

Tacit knowledge management is unrecorded.

Tacit knowledge is personal and hard to formulate and communicate.

Tacit knowledge is vulnerable to loss.

iii.   Expert knowledge

This is expertise that relies on knowledge to produce solutions.

Expert knowledge is also information woven into the mind of the expert for solving complex problems quickly and accurately.

iv.   Chunking knowledge

This type of knowledge is stored in an expert's long range memory as chunks. Knowledge chunking (compilation) enables experts to optimize their memory capacity and process information quickly. Chunks are groups of ideas or details that are stored and recalled together as a unit.

Challenges in building knowledge management:-

i.   Culture: Changing organizational culture is not an overnight exercise. People are reluctant to share their knowledge. People attitude have to be changed first.

ii.   Knowledge evaluation: The company has to give incentive so that employees agree to be evaluated.

iii.   Knowledge processing: Most companies do not realize the importance of the human element in knowledge management and therefore deny staff to know how decisions were reached.

iv.   Knowledge implementation: When it comes to knowledge management, an organization must commit to change, learning and innovating if it is to realize leadership in the market place.

Conditions in which knowledge management is important:-

i.   Business pressure on innovation.

ii.   Inter-organization enterprise e.g. mergers, takeovers etc.

iii.   Networked organizations that need to coordinate geographically dispersed groups.

iv.   Hyper competitive market places.

v.   Digitization of business environment and information technology revolution.

vi.   Concerns about the loss of knowledge due to increasing mobility, staff attrition and retirements.

Factors that contribute to the success of knowledge management:-

i.   Ensuring that company's vast knowledge resources are put to use.

ii.   Encouraging employees to use others' expertise contained in their data base.

iii.   Training employees on techniques of data collection to enrich organization data base.

iv.   Encouraging company experts to add their knowledge on the data base.

v.   Advising employees to donate information to the company.

vi.   Decentralizing or flattening the organization structure to allow decision making by team work.

vii.   Reducing control based management and encouraging management by results so that employees and teams can get their rightful credit for contribution to the company's profitability.

viii.   Revisiting the company's mission statements and ethics policy to demonstrate the company's new views about organizational values.

ix.   Opening lines of communication through periodic employee satisfaction surveys and transforming sessions.

x.   Assessing and improving employees responsibilities on a companywide basis; eliminating unnecessary directives of barriers.

xi.   Recognizing employees through bonus programs, knowledge employee of the month, on the employee bulletin board, or in the newspaper.

xii.   Installing an employee training programme especially geared for improving employee commitment to knowledge sharing.

Advantages of knowledge management:-

i.   Harnessing knowledge leads to considerable savings in the cost of operations.

ii.   It increases efficiency.

iii.   It improves the quality of both products and service.

iv.   Employees expertise is enhanced when they improve their skills to cope with the level of knowledge.

v.   Knowledge management enables the managers to promptly access the required information.

vi.   Knowledge management enables managers to plan effectively.

vii.   Knowledge management involves holistic view of the organization which lead to general improvement of the organization's operations.

viii.   Positive cumulative developments caused by knowledge management enhance corporate image of the organization.

Disadvantages of knowledge management:-

i.   Knowledge management relies on human skills for success

ii.   Knowledge management does not ensure success- employees must use it, but often they don't.

iii.   Employees decline to express their ideas to avoid staff in other companies have more knowledge.

iv.   To retrieve information, computers must be in operational state.

v.   Not all organizations use knowledge management. This makes some organizations be inaccessible hence negatively impact on those organizations that are isolated.

vi.   Development of knowledge management requires a high degree of expertise. However there is a shortage of these experts in the employment pool.

vii.   Employees have a tendency of refraining from using the knowledge that is available to them in the company leading to poor performance.

www.ingramcontent.com/pod-product-compliance
Lightning Source LLC
Chambersburg PA
CBHW070851180526
45168CB00005B/1771